The McCall's Book of

AFGHANS

BY THE EDITORS OF

McCall's Needlework & Crafts Publications

Simon and Schuster/The McCall Pattern Company/NEW YORK

Designed by Irving Perkins
Manufactured in the United States of America

1   2   3   4   5   6   7   8   9   10

Library of Congress Cataloging in Publication Data
Main entry under title:

The McCall's book of afghans.

1. Crocheting—Patterns.   2. Embroidery—Patterns.   3. Knitting—Patterns.
I. McCall's needlework & crafts.   TT825.M2   746.9′7   76-2400   ISBN 0-671-22224-4

Contents

Foreword 7

I Crocheted Afghans 9

One-Piece, 10; Border Afghan, 10; Golf Course Afghan, 13; Butterfly Afghan, 16; Folkways Afghan and Pillow, 20; Irish Afghan, 22; Stars and Bars Afghan, 24; Puff Pattern Afghan, 26; Radiant Star Afghan, 28; Open-Shell Afghan, 30; Rainbow Afghan, 31

Paneled, 32; Filet Crochet Afghan, 32; Stars and Stripes Afghan, 34; Fringed Jewel Afghan, 37; Bonny Plaid Carriage Cover, 38; "Stained Glass" Afghan, 40; Leaf Cluster Afghan, 42

Motifs, 44; Mohair Granny Squares Afghan, 44; Baby Afghan, 46; Jewel Tone Afghan, 48; Color Wheels Afghan, 50; Star Mosaic Afghan, 52; Pansy Afghan, 54; Bright Squares Afghan, 56; Gold-Edged Squares Afghan, 58; Dusty Rose Afghan, 60; Colonial Afghan, 62; Two-Tone Checkerboard Afghan and Pillow, 64; Butterfly Squares Afghan, 65; Nautical Afghan, 68

II Embroidered Afghans 71

Cameo Rose Afghan, 72; Folk Art Afghan and Pillow, 74; Floral Bouquet Afghan, 81; Florentine Afghan, 84; Nostalgia Afghan, 86; Treasure Chest Afghan, 90; Victorian Carriage Robe, 94; Seashells Afghan, 100; Birds in Flight Afghan, 103; Cowboy Afghan, 105

III Knitted Afghans 107

Pinwheel Afghan, 108; Striped Afghan and Pillows, 109; Quick-Knit Afghan, 110; Box-Pattern Afghan, 112; Cable Knit Afghan, 112; Navajo Blanket, 114; Flag Afghan, 116; Rose Afghan and Pillow, 118; Textured Stripes Afghan, 120; Double-Knit Afghan and Pillows, 122; Aran-Stripe Afghan, Pillows and Bolster, 125; Lily Pond Afghan or Bedspread, 131; Lace Pattern Afghan, 134; Leaf Pattern Afghan, 136

IV Special Techniques 139

Hairpin Lace Afghan, 140; Jigsaw Puzzle Afghan, 143; Broomstick Lace Afghan, 146; Daisy Afghan, 148; Rosette Afghan and Pompon Pillow, 150

V Abbreviations, Stitches and Additional How-To's 153

Foreword

What is an afghan? The dictionary says "a blanket or shawl of colored wool, knitted or crocheted in strips or squares which are joined by sewing or crocheting." Anyone who has ever seen an afghan, or owned one, or made one, knows it is far more than that. An afghan is a warm robe to snuggle in, to relax in, to dream in. It glows with color and is a thing of beauty and a delight to the eye wherever it goes. An afghan is an heirloom treasure, something to cherish, but to use, too, for more than one generation. An afghan is part of the American handcraft tradition, an expression of the love and joy of working with the hands, of making something useful and beautiful with the skill of your own fingers.

This book is a treasury of afghans for you to make and enjoy, some easy to do, some more difficult. There are crocheted afghans—many richly embroidered—and knitted afghans and some in special techniques combined with crochet. Just as the afghan you make will continue to give you joy, so will this book bring you pleasure whenever you open it.

The Editors of McCall's Needlework & Crafts Publications

Crocheted Afghans

One-Piece Afghans

Border Afghan

A glorious array of border patterns worked from a chart in single crochet and reverse single crochet creates this unique afghan. Use colors you have on hand, repeat the patterns you like.

SIZE: 44″ x 64″.

MATERIALS: Knitting worsted or Orlon yarn of same weight, 60 to 70 oz. in a variety of colors. The following approximate amounts are needed for afghan as shown: 10 oz. tan; 8 oz. brown; 6 oz. beige; 4 oz. each of red, black, medium blue, green, yellow; 3 oz. each of gray, purple, maroon; 2 oz. each of peach, rose, dark yellow, dark blue, light blue, dark red, aqua; 1 oz. dark green. Steel crochet hook No. 00.

GAUGE: 5 sc = 1″; 5 rows = 1″.

Note 1: Afghan is worked vertically from center pattern stripe out to last pattern stripe on side; second half is worked from center pattern stripe out to opposite side using same patterns and colors as first half. A border is then worked around entire afghan.

Note 2: Colors used in afghan are given in directions. Any desired colors may be used. Cut and join colors as needed.

Note 3: Work right side of afghan in sc; work wrong side in reverse sc. Or work all rows in sc from right side.

Note 4: On any row with 2 or more colors, begin row with all colors used on row. Work over colors not being used (lay unused colors along top of row, work sc as usual; unused colors will be hidden inside sts). When changing colors, work last sc or reverse sc of one color until there are 2 lps on hook, drop yarn to wrong side of work, finish st with new color. Continue in pattern, being sure to work over dropped color.

Reverse Sc: With yarn in front of hook, insert hook from back to front in st, catch yarn with hook, draw lp through to back of work, yo hook and through 2 lps on hook.

AFGHAN: FIRST HALF: With tan, ch 301.

Row 1 (right side): Sc in 2nd ch from hook and in each ch across—300 sc. Cut tan. Do not turn.

Row 2 (right side): With green, make lp on hook. Working over maroon and red, and beg in first sc at beg of row 1, work 1 green sc in each of first 3 sts, change to maroon (see Note 4); * work 3 maroon sc, change to red; work 1 red sc, change to maroon; work 1 maroon sc, change to green; work 3 green sc, change to maroon. Repeat from * across; end 1 maroon sc. See Chart 1; row

just worked is first row of chart, repeating from A to B across and ending from B to C once. Ch 1, turn.

Row 3 (wrong side): Working in reverse sc and working from chart, work from C to B once, then repeat from B to A across. Cut green. Ch 1, turn.

Row 4: Join yellow. Working in sc and working from chart, repeat from A to B across, ending from B to C once. Cut yellow. Ch 1, turn.

Row 5: Join green; repeat row 3. Ch 1, turn.

Row 6: Working in sc and working from chart, repeat from A to B across, ending from B to C once. Cut all colors. Do not turn.

Row 7 (right side): With tan, make lp on hook. Beg in first sc at beg of last row, work sc in each sc across; drop tan. Do not turn.

Row 8 (right side): With brown, make lp on hook. Beg in first sc at beg of last row, work sc in each sc across. Cut brown. Pick up tan; ch 1, turn.

Row 9 (wrong side): With tan, reverse sc in each sc across. Cut tan.

Following charts and working rows 7-9 between charts, work to top of Chart 11. Cut colors. Do not work rows 7-9 at top of Chart 11.

SECOND HALF: From right side, working on opposite side of starting ch, with brown, work sc in each ch across—300 sc. Cut brown. Do not turn.

With tan, work sc in each sc across. Cut tan. Do not turn. Beg with Chart 2, work as for first half of afghan.

FINISHING: Weave in yarn ends. Block afghan.

BORDER: Rnd 1: With tan, make lp on hook. From right side, sc in each sc and in end of each row around afghan, working 3 sc in each corner. Sl st in first sc. End off.

Rnd 2: With brown, sc in each sc around, 3 sc in sc at each corner. Sl st in first sc. End off.

Rnd 3: With tan, repeat rnd 2.

Rnd 4: With green, repeat rnd 2. Do not end off. Working from Chart 12, repeat from A to B around, increasing as necessary at corners to keep work flat and working added sts into pattern. When top of chart is reached, cut all colors but green, work 1 rnd green sc. End off.

THE
ULTIMATE
AFGHAN

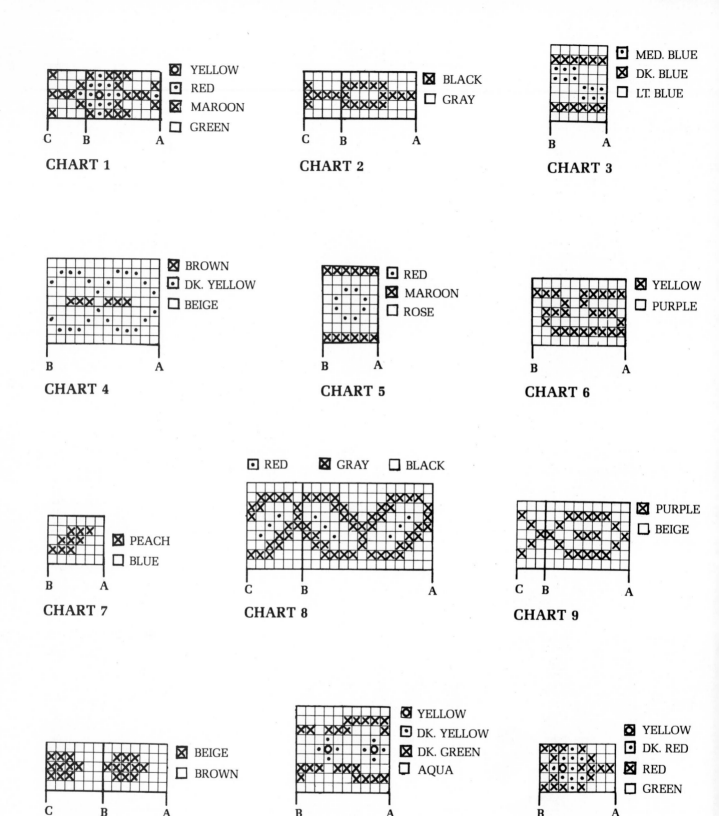

CHART 1

YELLOW
RED
MAROON
GREEN

C B A

CHART 2

BLACK
GRAY

C B A

CHART 3

MED. BLUE
DK. BLUE
LT. BLUE

B A

CHART 4

BROWN
DK. YELLOW
BEIGE

B A

CHART 5

RED
MAROON
ROSE

B A

CHART 6

YELLOW
PURPLE

B A

CHART 7

PEACH
BLUE

B A

RED GRAY BLACK

CHART 8

C B A

CHART 9

PURPLE
BEIGE

C B A

CHART 10

BEIGE
BROWN

C B A

CHART 11

YELLOW
DK. YELLOW
DK. GREEN
AQUA

B A

CHART 12

YELLOW
DK. RED
RED
GREEN

B A

Golf Course Afghan

A special afghan for the sporting man or woman features an 18-hole golf course complete with sandtraps, roughs, fairways and greens, all done in afghan-stitch crochet. Holes are marked with little red flags shown on page 14.

SIZE: 50" x 66", plus fringe.

MATERIALS: Knitting worsted, 8 4-oz. skeins light green, main color (MC), 4 skeins medium-bright green (MG), 3 skeins dark green (DG), 1 skein each red (R), light brown (LB), white (W), dark blue-green (BG), and medium blue (MB). Afghan hook size H. Small amount of red felt. White six-strand embroidery floss. Red sewing thread. Tapestry needle.

GAUGE: 4 sts = 1"; 3 rows = 1".

Note: Afghan is worked in one piece in afghan st, with pattern worked in.

TO CHANGE COLORS: Pick up number of lps of first color shown on chart, drop yarn; with new color, pick up specified number of lps. When the same color appears with no more than 4 sts of another color between, carry the first color across the back of your work. Join new colors as needed. Work off lps with matching color until there is 1 st left of that color, then change colors, picking up new color from underneath dropped strand to prevent hole in work. New color is drawn through 1 lp of previous color and 1 lp of new color. When a color is no longer needed, break off, leaving end long enough to be woven in on wrong side.

AFGHAN: Beg at lower edge, with MC, ch 196. Work in afghan st (see page 155), on 196 sts for 24 rows.

Row 25: Work 12 sts; place marker on work between 12th and 13th sts. Working from chart on page 15, work 73 more MC sts, work 1 BG st, work 98 MC sts. Place marker on work between st just worked and next st. Finish last 12 sts in MC. Keeping 12 sts each side of markers in MC for borders, work design on center 172 sts from chart. When top of chart is reached, end off all colors but MC. Work 25 more rows in MC. Sl st in each vertical bar across. End off.

FINISHING: With R and tapestry needle, work a running stitch along lines indicated by solid lines on chart, going under 1 row or st and over 1 row or st. From red felt, cut 18 flags. Using 2 strands of white six-strand embroidery floss, embroider numbers on flags in chain stitch. Sew flags to afghan with matching sewing thread.

FRINGE: Wind MC around a 16" cardboard. Cut at one end. Knot a 4-strand fringe in first st at bottom of afghan, then in every 4th st across.

Knot 8 strands of first fringe and 4 strands of 2nd fringe tog 1" below first row of knots. Knot 4 remaining strands of 2nd fringe and 4 strands of 3rd fringe tog 1" below first row of knots. Continue across, knotting 4 strands of 1 fringe with 4 strands of next fringe. Knot 8 strands of last fringe tog with 4 strands of next to last fringe. Trim.

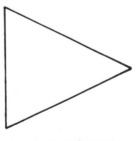

FLAG PATTERN

14

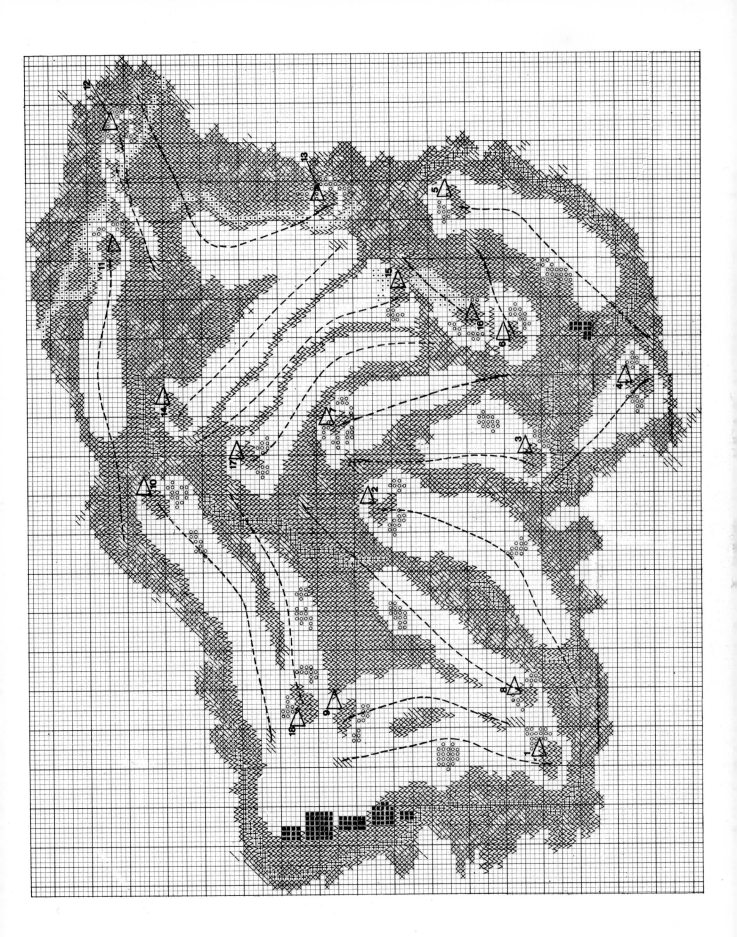

Butterfly Afghan

This exuberant fantasy of violets and butterfly wings is crocheted in one piece with the afghan stitch. The design is worked from a chart in four shades of soft green, two shades of blue, a touch of yellow. Knotted fringe trims both ends of the afghan. For those who have never done afghan stitch, directions include stitch details.

SIZE: 49″ x 63″, plus fringe.

MATERIALS: Knitting worsted, 4 4-oz. skeins of avocado, 3 skeins each of light lime, loden and fern moss, 2 skeins each of peacock and aqua, and 1 oz. of yellow. One or two afghan hooks, 14″ long, size 10. Yarn needle.

GAUGE: 4 sts = 1″; 3 rows = 1″.

AFGHAN: Beg at one end of afghan, with avocado, ch 192.

AFGHAN STITCH: Row 1: Keeping all lps on hook, pull up a lp in 2nd ch from hook and in each ch across—192 lps on hook. **Note:** If one hook seems too crowded, two hooks may be used, one for each half of afghan.

To Work Lps Off: Yo hook, pull through first lp, * yo hook, pull through next 2 lps, repeat from * across until 1 lp remains. Lp that remains on hook always counts as first st of next row.

Row 2: Keeping all lps on hook, sk first vertical bar (lp on hook is first st), pull up a lp under next vertical bar and under each vertical bar across to last st, make edge st by inserting hook under last vertical bar and lp at back of bar, pull up a lp. Work lps off as before.

Repeat row 2 until there are 6 rows of avocado. Beg with 7th row on chart (see pages 18-19), work afghan from chart, reading chart from right to left on all rows.

One row on chart equals both halves of one row of afghan st (pulling up lps and working them off).

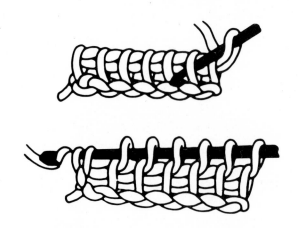

TO JOIN COLORS: On first half of row, pick up number of lps of first color shown on chart, drop yarn; with new color, pick up specified number of lps. When the same color appears with no more than 3 sts of another color between, the first color may be carried across the back of your work, but no more than 3 sts. Join new colors as needed. Work off lps with matching color until there is 1 st left of that color, then change colors, picking up new color from underneath dropped strand to prevent a hole in work. (New color is drawn through 1 lp of previous color and 1 lp of new color.)

When a color is no longer needed, break off, leaving an end long enough to be woven in on wrong side.

Work to top of chart (center of afghan), then work from top of chart back to row 1, omitting top row.

TO BIND OFF: Sl st in each vertical bar across.

Weave in all yarn ends on wrong side.

FRINGE: Cut avocado strands 24″ long, by winding yarn around a 12″ cardboard; cut through strands at one edge.

For first fringe at edge, hold 6 strands tog, fold in half.

From wrong side, insert hook in first ch at bottom edge, catch folded end of strands, pull loop through to wrong side, pull all 12 ends through loop; tighten knot. With 4 strands, repeat in every 4th ch across bottom edge, end with 6-strand fringe at other edge.

Take 8 of 12 ends hanging from first fringe, make knot in fringe 1½" below top row of knots. * Take 4 strands from one fringe and 4 strands from next fringe, knot strands tog 1½" below top row of knots, repeat from * across to last fringe; make knot in last 8 strands as for first knot. Repeat fringe on top edge, working under sl sts. Trim fringe evenly all around afghan.

☐ AVOCADO   ◹ LT. LIME   ◩ LODEN   ■ FERN MOSS

18

☒ PEACOCK   ⊟ AQUA   ◉ YELLOW

Folkways Afghan and Pillow

The Folkways afghan set is worked in an easy pattern: bands of double crochet and rows of shells. The square motifs are appliques; the zigzag design is crocheted on. The afghan is 42″ x 60″, plus cheery fringe; pillows are 14″ square.

MATERIALS: Orlon yarn of knitting-worsted weight, 9 2-oz. skeins winter white (W), 2 skeins each of medium blue (B), medium turquoise (T), maize (M) and avocado (A), 1 skein hot pink (P) for afghan. For pillows, 2 skeins W, 1 skein each of other 5 colors. 14″ square pillow forms. One yard unbleached muslin. Crochet hook size H.

GAUGE: 10 dc = 3″.

Afghan: With M, ch 147 loosely.

Row 1 (right side): Dc in 4th ch from hook, dc in each ch across—145 dc counting turning ch as 1 dc. Ch 3, turn.

Row 2: Sk first dc, dc in each dc across, dc in top of turning ch until 2 lps remain on hook, cut M; finish dc with W (always change colors in this way). Ch 1, turn.

Row 3: With W, sc in first dc, * sk 2 dc, 5 dc in next dc, sk 2 dc, sc in next dc, repeat from * across, change to B in last sc—24 shells. Ch 3, turn.

Row 4: With B, 2 dc in first sc, * sk 2 dc, sc in center dc of shell, 5 dc in next sc, repeat from * across, end 3 dc in last sc. Ch 1, turn.

Row 5: Sc in first dc, * shell in next sc, sc in center dc of next shell, repeat from * across, end sc in top of turning ch; change to W. Ch 3, turn.

Row 6: With W, repeat row 4.

Row 7: Sc in each dc and dc in each sc across. Change to T. Ch 3, turn.

Row 8: With T, sk first st, dc in each st across. Ch 3, turn.

Row 9: Repeat row 8. Change to W. Ch 3, turn.

Rows 10-23: With W, repeat row 8. At end of row 23, ch 1, turn.

Row 24: Repeat row 3. Change to M. Ch 3, turn.

Rows 25, 26: With M, repeat rows 4, 5. Change to W at end of row 26. Ch 3, turn.

Rows 27, 28: With W, repeat rows 4, 7. Change to T at end of row 28. Ch 3, turn.

Rows 29, 30: With T, repeat row 8. Change to W at end of row 30. Ch 3, turn.

Rows 31-41: Work in dc, working 7 rows W, 1 row B, 1 row W and 2 rows M. Repeat rows 3-41 twice more. End off.

Zigzag Trim: Join A with sc in top of first dc of row

32. Ch 4, sk first 3 dc on row 34, sc in top of next dc on row 34, * ch 4, sk 5 dc from last sc on row 32, sc in top of next dc, ch 4, sk 5 dc from last sc on row 34, sc in top of next dc, repeat from * across. Repeat on other two corresponding W stripes.

MOTIF (make 24): With P, ch 5, join with sl st to form ring.

Rnd 1: Ch 4, (dc in ring, ch 1) 7 times, sl st in 3rd ch of ch 4.

Rnd 2: Ch 1, sc in joining, (ch 9, sc in next dc, ch 2, sc in next dc) 4 times, sl st in first sc. End off P.

Rnd 3: With A, make lp on hook, * sc in next ch-9 lp, ch 3, sc in same lp, ch 4, dc in next ch-2 sp, ch 4, repeat from * around, sl st in first sc. End off.

Sew 8 motifs to each wide W stripe. With W, work 1 row sc along each side edge.

FRINGE: Cut 14″ strands of each color. Using 8 strands for each fringe, fold strands in half, draw folded end through lower edge between 2 dc, draw ends through the loop. Beg at side edge with W fringe, make fringes 9 dc apart in the following color sequences: B, A, T, P, M, W, A, B, P, T, M, W, A, T, P, B. Fringe other end.

Motif Pillow: With W, ch 51.

Row 1: Dc in 4th ch from hook (counts as 2 dc), dc in each ch across—49 dc. Ch 3, turn.

Rows 2-28: Sk first dc, dc in each dc across, dc in top of turning ch. Ch 3, turn. End off at end of row 28.

Make 5 motifs as for afghan. Sew to pillow as illustrated. Cover pillow form with muslin. Sew pillow top to one side. With 4 strands of A, make twisted cord 60″ long; see page 155. Sew cord around edge of pillow, hide knotted end inside muslin cover.

Striped Pillow: With W, ch 51.

Rows 1 and 2: Work as for Motif Pillow. At end of row 2, ch 1, turn.

Row 3: Repeat row 3 of afghan—8 shells. Change to M.

Rows 4 and 5: With M, repeat rows 4 and 5 of afghan. Change to W.

Rows 6 and 7: With W, repeat rows 6 and 7 of afghan. Change to T.

Rows 8 and 9: With T, repeat rows 8 and 9 of afghan. Change to W.

Rows 10-20: Repeat rows 31-41 of afghan.

Rows 21-29: Repeat rows 3-11 of afghan. End off. Work Zigzag Trim as for afghan on wide W stripe. Cover pillow form with muslin. Sew pillow top to one side. Cut 48 lengths of A 12″ long. Using 12 strands for each fringe, knot fringe in each corner.

Irish Afghan

The rich textures of Irish knits are borrowed for this afghan, all in crochet and worked in one piece.

SIZE: About 45″ x 61″, plus fringe.

MATERIALS: Knitting worsted, 17 4-oz. skeins. Aluminum crochet hooks sizes I and J.

GAUGE: 19 sc = 5″; 1 panel = 4″; 24 rows = 5″ (size I hook).

STITCH PATTERNS: Note: Do not work in stitch directly behind raised dc or double raised dc, or in eye of a cluster.

CLUSTER: (Yo hook, draw up a lp in st) 4 times, yo and draw through all 9 lps on hook. Ch 1 tightly to form eye. (Cluster is worked from wrong side but appears on right side.)

RAISED DC: Dc around upright bar of dc 1 row below, inserting hook behind dc from front to back to front, for ridge on right side.

DOUBLE RAISED DC: Holding back last lp of each dc on hook, make 2 dc around upright bar of st 1 row below, yo and through all 3 lps on hook.

POPCORN: 4 dc in st, drop lp off hook, insert hook in top of first dc, pick up dropped lp and pull through.

Note: This afghan is difficult to start. Once you have completed row 3 and "set" your stitches correctly, the work becomes relatively easy. Before starting afghan, make a swatch of one pattern to familiarize yourself with the stitches. Ch 28.

Row 1: Sc in 2nd ch from hook and in each ch across—27 sc.

Row 2: Sc in each of first 5 sts, cluster in next st, sc in each of next 15 sts, cluster in next st, sc in each of last 5 sts.

Row 3: Sc in each of first 3 sc; count off 3 sts on row 1 and work dc around next post (raised dc), sk the sc on row 2 behind the dc just made and make 1 sc in each of next 3 sts (be sure to work in the cluster st only once; do not work in the eye of the cluster), sk 3 sc on row 1 from last raised dc and work a raised dc around next st, sk the sc on row 2 behind the dc just made, sc in each of next 4 sc; sk 4 sc on row 1 from last raised dc and make double raised dc around next sc, sk the sc behind it and work 1 sc, sk 1 sc on row 1 and make another double raised dc, sk the sc behind it and work 4 sc; sk 4 sc on row 1 and work a raised dc around the next sc, sk the sc behind it, work 3 sc (the cluster st is the center st of these 3 sc), sk 3 sc on row 1 and work another raised dc around the next sc, sk the sc behind it, work sc in each of last 3 sts.

Beginning with row 4 of the afghan, work pattern without repeats on 27 sts. On all right-side rows from row 3 on, the raised dc's are worked around the previous raised dc's and the double raised dc's are worked around the double raised dc's.

AFGHAN: With I hook, ch 172 loosely.

Row 1: Sc in 2nd ch from hook and in each ch across—171 sc. Ch 1, turn each row.

Row 2 (wrong side): Sc in each of first 5 sts, (cluster in next st, sc in each of next 15 sts) 10 times; end cluster in next st, sc in each of last 5 sts.

Row 3 (right side): Sc in each of first 3 sc, * work dc around post of next sc 1 row below (row 1), sk next sc on row 2 (see Stitch Patterns: Note), sc in each of next 3 sts, dc around post of next sc 1 row below, sk next sc on row 2, sc in each of next 4 sc; holding back last lp of each dc on hook, make 2 dc around next sc 1 row below, yo and through 3 lps on hook, sk next sc on row 2, sc in next sc, sk 1 sc on row 1, make 2 dc around next sc as before, sk next sc on row 2, sc in each of next 4 sc, repeat from * across, end dc around post of next sc 1 row below, sc in each of next 3 sts, dc around post of next sc 1 row below, sc in each of last 3 sc.

Row 4: Sc in each of first 4 sts, (cluster in next sc, sc in next sc, cluster in next sc, sc in each of next 13 sts) 10 times, end cluster in next sc, sc in next sc, cluster in next sc, sc in each of last 4 sts.

Row 5: Sc in each of first 3 sc, * (raised dc in raised dc, sc in each of next 3 sts) twice, (double raised dc in double raised dc, sc in each of next 3 sc) twice, repeat from * across, end (raised dc in raised dc, sc in each of next 3 sts) twice.

Row 6: Repeat row 2.

Row 7: Sc in each of first 3 sc, * raised dc in raised dc, sc in each of next 3 sts, raised dc in raised dc, sc in each of next 2 sc, double raised dc in double raised dc, sc in each of next 5 sc, double raised dc in double raised dc, sc in each of next 2 sc, repeat from * across, end raised dc in raised dc, sc in each of next 3 sts, raised dc in raised dc, sc in each of last 3 sc.

Row 8: Repeat row 4.

Row 9: Sc in each of first 3 sc, * raised dc in raised dc, sc in each of next 3 sts, raised dc in raised dc, sc in next sc, double raised dc in double raised dc, sc in each of next 3 sc, popcorn in next sc, sc in each of next 3 sc, double raised dc in double raised dc, sc in next sc, repeat from * across, end raised dc in raised dc, sc in each of next 3 sts, raised dc in raised dc, sc in each of last 3 sc.

Row 10: Repeat row 2.

Row 11: Repeat row 7.
Row 12: Repeat row 4.
Row 13: Repeat row 5.
Row 14: Repeat row 2.
Row 15: Sc in each of first 3 sc, * raised dc in raised dc, sc in next 3 sts, raised dc in raised dc, sc in each of next 4 sc, double raised dc in double raised dc, sc in next sc, doubled raised dc in double raised dc, sc in each of next 4 sc, repeat from * across, end (raised dc in raised dc, sc in next 3 sts) twice.

Repeat rows 4-15 until 24 diamond patterns have been completed. End off. From right side, work 1 row sc across last row, end 2 sc in last st. Do not end off.

Edging: Rnd 1: Working down side of afghan, from right side, * sc in end st of next 2 rows, sk 1 row, repeat from * to corner, 3 sc in corner st, sc in each st across end to corner, 3 sc in corner; working up side, repeat from first * to beg of rnd, sl st in first sc.

Rnd 2: Join another strand of yarn. Using double strand and J hook, working from left to right, work sc in every other sc, inc at corners to keep work flat. Join; end.

FRINGE: Cut strands 14″ long. Hold 10 strands tog, fold in half. With hook, pull fold through edge of afghan, pull ends through loop; tighten knot. Knot a fringe in center of each diamond and cluster panel at each end and in each corner. Trim fringe.

23

Stars and Bars Afghan

An easy shell pattern forms red and white bands, worked in one piece, for the center of this afghan. The blue border is in the same stitch pattern. White crocheted stars are worked separately, sewn on. Picture courtesy of Bucilla Needlecraft.

SIZE: 54″ x 68″.

MATERIALS: Knitting worsted, 5 4-oz. skeins white (A), 4 skeins red (B) and 6 skeins blue (C). Crochet hook size G.

GAUGE: 2 shells and 2 spaces = 2″; 4 rows = 2″.

STRIPED CENTER: With A, ch 168 loosely.

Row 1 (right side): Work 2 dc in 4th ch from hook, * sk 3 ch, 3 dc in next ch (1 shell made), repeat from * to end—42 shells.

Row 2: Ch 3 loosely, turn; * 3 dc in next sp between shells, repeat from *, end with dc in top of ch 3—41 shells.

Note: Ch 3 at beg of each row counts as 1 dc.

Row 3: Ch 3, turn; 2 dc in sp before first shell, 1 shell in each sp to end—42 shells.

Row 4: Same as row 2. End off.

Row 5: From right side, with lp of B on hook, sl st into sp before first shell, ch 3, 2 dc in same sp, 1 shell in each sp to end.

Rows 6, 7 and 8: Continuing with B, work same as for rows 2, 3 and 4.

With A, repeat last 4 rows.

Continue in this manner, alternating 4 rows A and 4 rows B until 13 A stripes and 12 B stripes have been completed, end on wrong side at upper edge.

BORDER: Rnd 1: From right side, beg at upper right corner, with lp of C on hook, with care to keep work flat, sl st into corner sp, ch 3, 2 dc in same sp (one half corner), shell in each sp to within corner, shell, ch 3, shell, all in corner sp, shell in each sp along side edge, shell, ch 3, shell, all in corner; continue around, working opposite edges to correspond, end with shell in same sp as first shell, ch 3, join with sl st in top of ch 3 of first shell to complete corner.

Rnd 2: Turn, sl st in center of corner sp, ch 3, turn, 2 dc in same sp for half corner, shell in each sp to within corner, shell, ch 3, shell in corner, complete rnd same as for rnd 1.

Repeat rnd 2 until there are 13 rnds for border. End off.

FINISHING: Block to given measurements.

STARS (make 40): With A, ch 5, join with sl st in first ch to form a ring.

Rnd 1: Ch 2, work 14 hdc in ring, join with sl st in top of ch 2.

Rnd 2 (points): * Ch 7, turn; sl st in 2nd ch from hook, sc in next ch, hdc in next ch, dc in each of next 2 ch, tr in next ch, sk 2 hdc of rnd 1, sl st in next hdc; repeat from * 4 times. End off.

Sew 11 stars on each side border and 9 stars each on upper and lower borders, at each point and center, as illustrated.

TASSELS (make 4): Wind C around a 12″ cardboard about 50 times. With double strand tie tightly and securely through loops at one end, leaving ends of yarn to sew tassel to afghan. Cut loops at opposite end. Beg about 1½″ below tie, wind C around tassel about 15 times. Fasten tightly and securely.

Trim evenly.

Sew one tassel to each corner.

Puff Pattern Afghan

A creamy, quick-to-crochet afghan combines rows of single crochet with puffs and bands of a nubbly pattern stitch. Four strands of knitting worsted and a giant hook create the texture. Knotted fringe goes all around.

SIZE: 40″ x 60″, plus fringe.

MATERIALS: Knitting worsted, 19 4-oz. skeins. Jumbo crochet hook size Q.

GAUGE: 5 sts = 4″; 4 rows of sc = 3″ (4 strands of yarn).

AFGHAN: Beg at one long edge, using 4 strands of yarn tog, ch 76.

Row 1: Sc in 2nd ch from hook and in each ch across—75 sc. Ch 1, turn.

Row 2: Sc in each sc across. Check gauge; piece should measure 60″ across. Ch 1, turn each row.

Row 3 (right side): Sc in each of first 3 sc, * pull up a lp in next st, (yo hook, pull up a lp in same st) twice, (yo hook and through 2 lps on hook) twice, yo hook and through remaining 4 lps (puff st made); bringing puff st toward you, sc in each of next 3 sc, repeat from * across, end sc in each of last 3 sc.

Rows 4-6: Sc in each st across.

Row 7: Pull up a long lp in first sc, yo hook, pull up a long lp in next sc, yo and through first lp on hook, yo and through 4 lps on hook, * pull up a long lp in last sc worked, yo hook, pull up a long lp in next sc, yo and through first lp on hook, yo and through 4 lps, repeat from * across—74 sts. Ch 2, turn.

Row 8: Sc in 2nd ch from hook, sc in each st across—75 sc.

Row 9: Repeat row 7.

Row 10: Repeat row 8.

Rows 11 and 12: Work even in sc.

Row 13: Repeat row 3.

Rows 14-17: Work even in sc.

Rows 18-23: Repeat rows 7 and 8 alternately.

Rows 24-33: Work even in sc.

Rows 34-39: Repeat rows 7 and 8 alternately.

Rows 40-42: Work even in sc.

Row 43: Repeat row 3.

Rows 44-46: Work even in sc.

Rows 47-50: Repeat rows 7 and 8 alternately.

Rows 51-52: Work even in sc.

Row 53: Repeat row 3.

Rows 54-55: Work even in sc.

Row 56: Sl st loosely in each st across. End off.

FINISHING: Work 1 row of sl st loosely across each end of afghan.

FRINGE: Wind yarn around 12″ cardboard. Cut at one edge for 24″ strands. Holding 6 strands tog, fold in half; with crochet hook, pull loop through st on edge, pull 12 ends through loop; tighten knot. Knot a fringe in every other st on all four sides. Separate each fringe into two groups of 6 ends. Knot tog 6 ends of one fringe to 6 ends of adjacent fringe about ¾″ below first row of knots. Knot ends tog once more in same manner ¾″ below 2nd row of knots. Trim ends evenly.

Radiant Star Afghan

This star-shaped afghan is crocheted all in one piece, starting at the center with a five-sided figure. White points are added to the five sides, then the whole star is edged with a deep border of red and navy. Stitches are simple, alternating rounds of double crochet and single crochet. Red, white, and blue fringe adds a sporty finish.

SIZE: 65″ from point to opposite corner between points.

MATERIALS: Knitting worsted, 5 4-oz. skeins white, 3 skeins each of red and navy. Crochet hook size G.

GAUGE: 4 dc = 1″.

AFGHAN: Beg at center, with white, ch 4.

Rnd 1: 14 dc in 4th ch from hook, sl st to top of ch 4 to join rnd—15 dc.

Rnd 2: Ch 3 (counts as 1 dc), 2 dc in same ch with sl st, * 2 dc in each of 2 dc, 3 dc in next dc, repeat from * 3 times, 2 dc in each of last 2 dc—35 dc. Join each rnd with sl st.

Rnd 3: Sl st in next dc, ch 1, 3 sc in same dc, (sc in 6 dc, 3 sc in next dc) 4 times, sc in 6 dc.

Rnd 4: Sl st in next sc (center sc of 3-sc group), ch 3, 2 dc in same st, (dc in 8 sc, 3 dc in center sc of 3-sc group) 4 times, dc in 8 sc.

Rnd 5: Sl st in next st, ch 3, 2 dc in same st, (dc in each st to center st at point, 3 dc in center st) 4 times, dc in each remaining st.

Rnd 6: Sl st in next st, ch 1, 3 sc in same st, (sc in each st to center st at point, 3 sc in center st) 4 times, sc in each remaining st.

Rnds 7-30: Continue in this manner, repeating rnd 5 twice, rnd 6 once (2 rnds dc, 1 rnd sc), end with sc rnd.

Star Points: Row 1: Sl st in next st, ch 3, dc in each st across to next point, dc in point—64 dc. Ch 2, turn.

Row 2: Sk first and next st, dc in each st across to 2 sts from end, sk next st, dc in last st—1 st dec each end. Ch 1, turn.

Row 3: Sc in each dc across. Ch 2, turn.

Row 4: Sk first and next st, dc in each st across to 2 sts from end, sk next st, dc in last st. Ch 2, turn.

Row 5: Sk first and next st, dc in each st across to 2 sts from end, sk next st, dc in last st. Ch 1, turn. Repeat rows 3-5, decreasing 2 sts each dc row, until 4 dc remain. Ch 2, turn.

Last Row: Yo hook, pull up a lp in next st, yo and through 2 lps on hook, yo hook, pull up a lp in last st, yo and through 2 lps, yo and through 3 lps on hook. End off.

Join white in same st on rnd 30 as last st of row 1 of star point. Ch 3, dc in each st across to next point, dc in point—64 dc. Ch 2, turn. Work as for first point from row 2. Work next 3 points the same. When 5th point is completed, do not end off. Ch 1, work 1 row sc around entire piece, working 2 sc in side of each dc row, 1 sc in side of each sc row, skipping 2 sts at inner corners of points, and working 3 sc at each point. Join; end off.

Red Border: Rnd 1: Join red in center st at one point, ch 3, 2 dc in same st, * dc in each sc to inner corner, sk 2 sts, dc in each sc to next point, 3 dc in point, repeat from * around, end sl st to top of ch 3.

Rnd 2: Sl st in next st, ch 3, 2 dc in same st, * dc in each dc to inner corner, sk 2 sts, dc in each dc to next point, 3 dc in point, repeat from * around, end sl st to top of ch 3.

Rnd 3: Sl st in next st, ch 1, 3 sc in same st, * sc in each dc to inner corner, sk 2 sts, sc in each dc to next point, 3 sc in point, repeat from * around, end sl st in first sc.

Rnds 4-11: Continue in this manner, working 2 rnds dc, 1 rnd sc, decreasing 2 sts at corners, increasing 2 sts at points; end with 2nd dc rnd. End off.

Navy Border: Rnds 12-21: With navy, beg with sc rnd, work as for red border.

FINISHING: Cut yarn into 5″ lengths. Using strands singly, knot fringe in each st around edge, having * 4 white fringes, 1 red fringe, 4 white fringes, 1 navy fringe, repeat from * around. Steam-press points.

Open-Shell Afghan

This shell-stitch afghan is worked in shades of yellow and brown that deepen in tone from the center out, and is crocheted in one large rectangle. Make it of knitting worsted or Orlon yarn of the same thickness, in five colors or as many as you like.

SIZE: 42″ x 60″.

MATERIALS: Knitting worsted or Orlon 4-ply knitting yarn, 1 4-oz. skein each of light yellow (A), dark yellow (B) and orange (C), 2 skeins each of light brown (D) and dark brown (E). Crochet hook size J or 9.

GAUGE: 2 shells = 3″; 5 rnds = 4″.

AFGHAN: Beg at center, with A, ch 52 loosely to measure 20″.

Rnd 1: Dc in 4th ch from hook, ch 2, 2 dc in same ch (1 shell), ch 2; in same ch make 2 dc, ch 2 and 2 dc for another shell, * sk 3 ch, shell of 2 dc, ch 2, 2 dc in next ch, repeat from * across, end shell in last ch, ch 2, shell in same last ch; working on opposite side of starting ch, make a shell in every ch that has a shell on first half of rnd, join with sl st in top of ch 3.

Rnd 2: Sl st in next dc and in each of 2 ch of ch-2 sp, ch 3; in same ch-2 sp make dc, ch 2 and 2 dc for starting shell, sk next ch-2 sp; in next ch-2 sp of next shell make 2 shells with ch 2 between shells for a corner, shell in ch-2 sp of each shell to next corner, 2 shells with ch 2 between shells in next corner, sk next ch-2 sp, 2 shells with ch 2 between shells in 4th corner, shell in ch-2 sp of each shell to starting shell, make shell in same sp as starting shell, ch 2, join to top of ch 3. Remove hook from lp; insert hook under ch 2, bring lp through to right side.

Rnd 3: Ch 3; make starting shell in same sp, shell in each ch-2 sp around, including ch-2 sp at each corner, join to top of ch 3. End off A.

Rnd 4: With B, make starting shell in any corner, work in shell pat around, making 2 shells with ch 2 between shells in each corner, end shell in same sp as starting shell, ch 2, join to top of ch 3. Drop lp and pull through to right side in ch-2 sp.

Rnd 5: Work in shell pat around, making 2 shells (without ch 2 between shells) in ch-2 sp at each corner, end shell in same sp as starting shell; join to top of ch 3. Drop lp and draw it through to right side between last dc and ch 3.

Rnd 6: Ch 3, make starting shell in same place, work in shell pat around, making 1 shell in each corner shell and 1 shell in each corner between 2 corner shells. Join to top of ch 3. Sl st to ch-2 sp at corner.

Repeat rnds 5 and 6 for pattern. Work 2 more rnds of B (5 B rnds). End off B. Always joining new color at a corner, work 5 rnds C, 6 rnds D and 6 rnds E. Run in yarn ends.

Rainbow Afghan

To create this glowing afghan—shown here in black and white— follow our color suggestions for a rainbow effect, or use colors of your choice. Afghan is crocheted like a giant granny motif.

SIZE: 50″ square.

MATERIALS: Knitting worsted, 1 oz. each of light yellow and emerald green, 2 oz. each of medium yellow, dark yellow, orange, watermelon pink, dark rose red, dark old rose, lilac, purple, medium blue, dark blue. Crochet hook size H.

GAUGE: 3 pats = 4″.

AFGHAN: Beg at center with light yellow, ch 6. Sl st in first ch to form ring.

Rnd 1: Ch 3 (counts as 1 dc), 2 dc in ring, (ch 2, 3 dc in ring) 3 times, ch 2, sl st to top of ch 3, sl st in each of next 2 dc, sl st in ch-2 sp.

Rnd 2: Ch 3, 2 dc in ch-2 sp, ch 2, 3 dc in same ch-2 sp, (ch 1, 3 dc, ch 2, 3 dc in next ch-2 sp) 3 times, ch 1, sl st to top of ch 3, sl st in each of next 2 dc, sl st in ch-2 sp.

Rnd 3: Ch 3, 2 dc in ch-2 sp, ch 2, 3 dc in same ch-2 sp, (ch 1, 3 dc in next sp, ch 1, 3 dc, ch 2, 3 dc in next corner sp) 3 times, ch 1, 3 dc in next sp, ch 1, sl st to top of ch 3, sl st in each of next 2 dc, sl st in ch-2 sp. End off.

Rnd 4: With medium yellow, make lp on hook, join with sl st in any corner sp, ch 3, 2 dc in same sp, ch 2, 3 dc in same sp, * (ch 1, 3 dc in next sp) twice, ch 1, 3 dc, ch 2, 3 dc in corner sp, repeat from * twice, (ch 1, 3 dc in next sp) twice, ch 1, sl st to top of ch 3, sl st in each of next 2 dc, sl st in ch-2 sp.

Work as for rnd 4 throughout, having 1 more group of 3 dc on each side every rnd. Work 2 more rnds of medium yellow, 3 rnds dark yellow, 3 rnds orange, 3 rnds watermelon pink, 3 rnds dark rose red, 2 rnds dark old rose, 3 rnds lilac, 3 rnds purple, 2 rnds medium blue and 2 rnds dark blue.

Edging: With green, work 1 rnd sc, working 1 sc in each dc and ch around. End off.

Paneled Afghans

Filet Crochet Afghan

Five identical strips of filet crochet make this lacy and lightweight coverlet especially easy to crochet. Each panel is edged round with double crochet, then the panels are sewn together. Picture courtesy of Bucilla Needlecraft.

SIZE: 50" x 68".

MATERIALS: Wool and Shetland wool, 15 2-oz. skeins. Crochet hook size F.

GAUGE: 7 sps = 4½"; 2 rows = 1".

AFGHAN STRIP (make 5): Ch 47 for lower edge.

Row 1 (wrong side): Work 1 dc in 8th ch from hook, * ch 2, sk 2 ch, dc in next ch, repeat from * to end—14 sps.

Row 2: Ch 5, turn, sk first sp, dc in next dc, * ch 2, dc in next dc, repeat from *, end with dc in 3rd ch—14 sps. Repeat row 2 until there are 8 rows.

Row 9: Ch 5, turn, sk first sp, dc in next dc, ch 2, dc in next dc, ch 2, dc in next dc (3 sps made), * 2 dc in next sp, dc in next dc (1 block), repeat from * 7 times, ch 2, dc in next dc, ch 2, dc in next dc, ch 2, dc in 3rd ch (last 3 sps made)—6 sps and 8 blocks.

Row 10: Ch 5, turn, work first 3 sps as before, dc in each of next 24 dc, work last 3 sps.

Row 11: Ch 5, turn, work first 3 sps, dc in each of next 3 dc, * ch 2, sk 2 dc, dc in next dc, repeat from * 5 times, dc in each of next 3 dc, work last 3 sps.

Row 12: Ch 5, turn, work first 3 sps, dc in each of next 3 dc, ch 2, dc in next dc, * 2 dc in next sp, dc in next dc, repeat from * 3 times, ch 2, dc in each of next 4 dc, work last 3 sps.

Row 13: Ch 5, turn, work first 3 sps, dc in each of next 3 dc, ch 2, dc in each of next 13 dc, ch 2, dc in each of next 4 dc, work last 3 sps.

Repeat row 13, 4 times.

Row 18: Ch 5, turn, work first 3 sps, dc in each of next 3 dc, ch 2, dc in next dc, * ch 2, sk 2 dc, dc in next dc, repeat from * 3 times, ch 2, dc in each of next 4 dc, work last 3 sps.

Row 19: Ch 5, turn, work first 3 sps, dc in each of next 3 dc, * 2 dc in next sp, dc in next dc, repeat from * 5 times, dc in each of next 3 dc, work last 3 sps.

Row 20: Repeat row 10.

Row 21: Ch 5, turn, work first 3 sps, * ch 2, sk 2 dc, dc in next dc, repeat from * 7 times, work last 3 sps.

Rows 22-28: Repeat row 2, then repeat rows 9-28 5 times, end on right side. End off. Mark last row for upper edge of afghan.

Edging: With lp of yarn on hook, from right side, beg in st at upper right corner, ch 3, 4 dc in same st for corner; with care to keep work flat, working along upper edge, dc in first sp, * dc in dc, 2 dc in next sp, dc in dc, dc in next sp, repeat from *, end with 2 dc in last sp, 5 dc in corner st; along side edge work dc in each sp and dc in base of end st of each row; continue around, working 5 dc in each corner, lower edge same as upper edge and 2nd side edge same as first side edge, join with sl st in top of ch 3. End off.

FINISHING: Block each strip to 10" x 68".

Having marked edges of strips at same end, matching rows and keeping seams elastic, from right side sew strips tog, through top lps only. Steam lightly.

Stars and Stripes Afghan

Alternating blue and white star motifs, joined together in the crochet, form an undulating pattern across striped afghan. Red bands of solid and openwork crochet are added to the upper and lower edges of each star strip, then strips are sewn together for a waving flag effect. Giant tassels trim the afghan top and bottom. Picture courtesy of Bucilla Needlecraft.

SIZE: 42″ x 64″, without tassels.

MATERIALS: Knitting worsted, 6 4-oz. skeins navy (A), 3 skeins white (B) and 7 skeins red (C). Crochet hook size G.

GAUGE: Center of full star = 1¼″. Star, point to point = 2½″.

Note: Ch 3 at beg of centers counts as 1 dc.

FIRST STAR STRIP: Half Star for Right Edge: Center: With A, ch 1 loosely, ch 3 more (see Note), work 6 dc and 3 tr in first ch—10 sts. End off.

Points: From right side, with lp of A on hook, sl st in top of ch 3, (ch 4 for base of point, sc in 2nd ch from hook for tip of point, dc in next ch, tr in next ch, sk next 2 dc on center, sl st in next dc to complete point) twice. End off. Mark last point made.

First Full Star: Center: With B, ch 1 loosely, ch 3 more, work 14 dc in first ch, sl st in top of ch 3—15 sts.

Note: Centers of all full stars are made in this manner.

First Point: Ch 4, join to marked point of half star in following manner: drop lp from hook; from right side, insert hook in sc at tip of point and draw dropped lp through, * work sc in 2nd ch from hook for tip of point, dc in next ch, tr in next ch, sk 2 dc on center, sl st in next dc to complete point *.

2nd Point: Ch 4, join to remaining point of half star as before, repeat between *'s of first point once.

3rd, 4th, 5th Points: (Ch 4, repeat between *'s of first point once) 3 times. End off. Mark last point for 5th point. Mark half star for right edge of strip.

Note: Star on which you are working will always be joined to 5th then 4th points of previous full star. At end of each star, mark last point made for 5th point.

2nd Full Star: With A, make center as on first full star.

First Point: Ch 4, * work sc in 2nd ch from hook for tip of point, dc in next ch, tr in next ch, sk 2 dc on center, sl st in next dc to complete point *.

2nd Point: Ch 4, join to 5th point of previous star as before, repeat between *'s of first point once.

3rd Point: Ch 4, join to 4th point of previous star, repeat between *'s of first point once.

4th and 5th Points: Same as first point. End off.

3rd Full Star: With B, make center as on first full star.

First Point: Ch 4, join to 5th point of previous star and complete point as before.

2nd Point: Ch 4, join to 4th point of previous star and complete point.

3rd, 4th, 5th Points: Same as for first point on 2nd full star.

Repeat 2nd and 3rd full stars 8 times—one half star in A and 19 alternating full stars, beg and ending with B.

Half Star for Left Edge: Note: Ch 4 at beg of center counts as 1 tr.

Center: With A, ch 1 loosely, ch 4 more, work 2 tr and 7 dc in first ch—10 sts. End off.

Points: From right side, with loop of A on hook, sk first 3 sts, sl st in top of first dc, ch 4, join to 5th point of previous star and complete point, ch 4, join to 4th point of previous star, complete point and end off.

Note: Each row of border is worked from right side with C and fastened off at end.

Upper Border: Row 1: From right side, with lp of C on hook, beg at base of upper point of half star from marked right edge, work sc in tr, sc in dc, sc in sc; (* on next star, work hdc in sc at tip of point, dc in next dc, dc in next tr, tr in sl st between points; on next point, work dc each in next tr, dc and sc, 3 dc in ch 1 at tip of point, dc each in next sc, dc and tr, tr in sl st between points; on next point, work dc in tr, dc in dc, hdc in sc *; on point of next star, work sc each in sc, dc and tr, sc in sl st between points; on next point work sc each in tr, dc and sc) 9 times; repeat between *'s once; on upper point of half star for left edge, work sc each in sc, dc and tr—239 sts. End off.

Note: Ch 2 at beg of rows 2 and 4 is not counted as a st.

Row 2: From right side, with lp on hook, sl st in first st, ch 2, sk next st, dc in next st, dc in each of next 8 sts, 3 dc in next st (the center st of 3 dc of previous row—an inc), dc in each of next 9 sts; († * yo, draw up a lp in next st, yo and through only 2 lps *, sk next 3 sts, repeat between *'s once, yo and through remaining 3 lps (a dec), dc in each of next 9 sts, 3 dc in next st as before †, dc in

34

each of next 9 sts) 8 times; repeat between †'s once, dc in each of next 8 sts; repeat between *'s once, sk next st, repeat between *'s once, yo and through remaining 3 lps on hook—219 sts. End off.

Note: Ch 4 at beg of row counts as 1 dc, ch 1 (2 sts).

Row 3: From right side, with lp on hook, skipping ch 2 at beg of row, sl st in first dc, ch 4, sk 1 dc, dc in next dc, * ch 1, sk 1 dc, dc in next dc *; repeat between *'s twice, † ch 1, sk next st, dc, ch 3, dc all in next st (center st of previous inc—an inc), repeat between *'s 4 times †, (ch 1, sk next dc, ** yo, draw up a lp in next st, yo and through 2 lps on hook **, sk dec on previous row, repeat between **'s once, yo and through remaining 3 lps (a dec), repeat between *'s 4 times, repeat between †'s once) 9 times, ch 1, sk next dc, dc in last st—241 sts. End off.

Row 4: From right side, with lp on hook, sl st in 3rd ch of ch 4 at beg of row, ch 2, dc in next dc, * ch 1, dc in next dc *, repeat between *'s 3 times, ch 1, sk 1 ch, dc, ch 3, dc all in next ch (center ch of previous inc), repeat between *'s 4 times, (ch 1, ** yo, draw up a lp in next dc, yo and through 2 lps on hook **, sk dec on previous row, repeat between **'s once, yo and through remaining 3 lps, repeat between *'s 4 times, ch 1, sk 1 ch, dc, ch 3, dc all in next ch as before, repeat between *'s 4 times) 9 times, ch 1, repeat between **'s twice, yo and through 3 remaining lps—241 sts. End off.

Mark last row for upper border.

Lower Border: Row 1: From right side, working along opposite edge of star strip, beg on center of half star, with lp of C on hook, sl st in top of ch 4, ch 3, dc in same st, dc in each of next 2 tr, tr in sl st; on point, work dc in tr, dc in dc, hdc in sc; on point of next star work sc each in sc, dc and tr, sc in sl st between points; on next point work sc each in tr, dc and sc; repeat between( ) of row 1 for upper border 9 times; on point of half star work hdc in sc, dc in dc, dc in tr, tr in sl st; on center, work dc in each of next 2 sts, 2 dc in last st—239 sts. End off.

Row 2: From right side, with lp on hook, sl st in top of ch 3 at beg of row, ch 3, dc in same st, dc in each of next 8 sts, repeat between ( ) of row 2 for upper border 9 times, work 1 more dec as before, dc in each of next 8 sts, 2 dc in last st—219 sts. End off.

Row 3: From right side, with lp on hook, sl st in top of ch 3 at beg of row, ch 4, dc in same st, ch 1, dc in next st, * ch 1, sk 1 dc, dc in next dc *, repeat between *'s twice, repeat between ( ) of row 3 for upper border 9 times, ch 1, sk next dc, work 1 more dec as before, repeat between *'s 4 times, ch 1, dc, ch 1, dc all in last st—241 sts. End off.

Row 4: From right side, with lp on hook, sl st in 3rd ch of ch 4 at beg of row, ch 4, dc in same st,* ch 1, dc in next dc *, repeat between *'s 3 times, repeat between ( ) of row 4 for upper border 9 times, ch 1, work 1 more dec as before, repeat between *'s 4 times, ch 1, dc, ch 1, dc all in last st—241 sts. End off. Block to measurements given in diagram below.

2nd Star Strip: Work same as for first star strip, reversing colors—beg and ending with half stars in B; upper and lower borders in C.

Joining: Carefully pin edge of upper border of first strip and edge of lower border of 2nd strip tog, pinning center of ch 3 at outer corner of one border to dec at inner corner of next border. With C, taking care to keep

seams elastic, matching sts, sew tog through top lps only. Repeat first and 2nd strips and joining until 10 strips have been completed. Mark 10th strip for upper edge of afghan.

Edging: Left Side: Row 1: From right side, beg at upper left corner, with lp of B on hook, sl st in edge of first row; working along left edge, with care to keep work flat, * ch 3, sl st in edge of next row *, repeat between *'s once, † ch 3, sl st in sl st of point, ch 3, sl st in ch 1 of center of half star, repeat between *'s 8 times, repeat from † across, end with repeat between *'s 5 times with last sl st in edge of last row. End off.

Row 2: From right side, with lp of A on hook, beg at upper left corner, sl st in edge of first row to right of first st of row 1, * ch 3, sl st in next lp, repeat from * across, end with last sl st to left of last st of row 1—100 lps. End off.

Right Side: Row 1: From right side, beg at lower right corner, with lp of B on hook, sl st in edge of first row; working along right edge, with care to keep work flat, * ch 3, sl st in edge of next row *; repeat between *'s 3 times, † ch 3, sl st in ch 1 of center of half star, ch 3, sl st in first st of point, repeat between *'s 8 times; repeat from † across, end with repeat between *'s 3 times with last sl st in edge of last row. End off.

Row 2: Same as row 2 for left side. Block.

Tassels (make 21): Wind A around a 10″ cardboard about 60 times. With double strand of A, tie tightly through loops at one end, leaving ends of yarn to sew tassels to afghan. Cut loops at other end. Beg at about 2½″ below tied end, wind double strand B around tassel about 20 times to cover about 1″ for neck. Fasten securely. With double strand of A, wind around center of neck, winding twice. Fasten securely. Trim tassels evenly. Sew 1 tassel to each point along upper and lower edges of afghan.

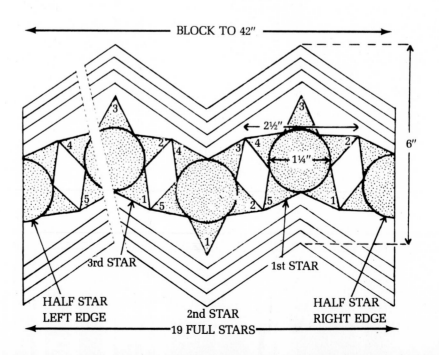

Fringed Jewel Afghan

This contemporary afghan in jewel tones of sapphire, emerald, and turquoise can be made by the beginner. The background is crocheted in easy-to-handle 7" x 9" pieces and fringed with two blues, two greens. Blocks, then strips, are sewn together to form a continuous fringed pattern.

SIZE: About 54" x 63".

MATERIALS: Knitting worsted, 64 oz. royal blue, main color (MC), 6 oz. each of emerald green (EG) and dark turquoise (DT), 5 oz. light emerald green (LG). Plastic crochet hooks, sizes I and F. Tapestry needle.

GAUGE: 10 sc = 3"; 7 rows = 2" (sc ridge rows, size I hook).

Note: Motifs, 7" x 9", are crocheted and fringed separately, then sewed tog. For afghan approximately 54" x 63", make 54 motifs.

MOTIF: With MC and size I hook, ch 30 loosely to measure about 9". **Row 1:** Sc in 2nd ch from hook and in each remaining ch—29 sc. Ch 1, turn.

Row 2: Sc in each sc across. Ch 1, turn.

Row 3 (ridge row): Working through back lp of sts only, sc in each st across. Ch 1, turn.

Row 4: Working through both lps of sts, sc in each st. Ch 1, turn.

Rows 5-24: Repeat rows 3 and 4 alternately 10 times—11 ridge rows. Cut yarn, leaving a 15" end for sewing.

FRINGE: Wind all four colors of yarn separately or together over a 1¾" cardboard. Cut through yarn at one edge to make strands for fringe.

To Knot Fringe: Insert size F hook from bottom up through 1 free lp on ridge row, fold one strand of yarn cut for fringe in half over hook; pull folded end through st to form a loop on hook, pull 2 ends of strand down through loop; pull ends to tighten knot.

Fringe Pattern: Row 1: Beg at lower right corner of motif, knot a fringe in each of 29 sts of first ridge row, following row 1 of chart for colors.

Row 2: Skip next ridge row. Working in next ridge row and following row 2 of chart, knot fringe across.

Row 3: Skip next ridge row. Working in next ridge row and following row 3 of chart, knot fringe across.

Skipping 1 ridge row between fringe rows, repeat rows 1, 2 and 3 once more.

FINISHING: Sew 9 motifs tog along 9" width, one above the other, with fringe going in one direction, using ends left for sewing. Make 5 more strips in same way. Sew strips tog side by side. With MC, work 1 row of sc around afghan, working 1 sc in each st at top and bottom of afghan, 1 sc in end of each row at sides, 3 sc in each corner. Join with sl st to first sc; end off. Trim fringe evenly to 1¼" length.

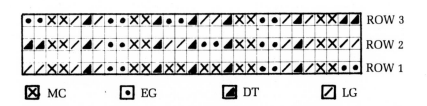

ROW 3
ROW 2
ROW 1

☒ MC   ⊡ EG   ◢ DT   ◿ LG

37

Bonny Plaid Carriage Cover

A bonny plaid carriage cover for baby's promenades is crocheted in two tones of blue with white, then fringed in all three colors. The strips are worked in half double crochet and sewn together to create a subtle woven effect.

SIZE: About 27" x 33" with fringe.

MATERIALS: Knitting worsted, 5 1-oz. skeins white (W); 7 skeins light blue (LB) and 6 skeins medium blue (MB). Steel crochet hook No. 00.

GAUGE: Each panel 2¼" wide; 5 pat rows (1 square) = 2¼".

PATTERN: Row 1: 2 hdc in 3rd ch from hook (1 pat made), * sk 1 ch, 2 hdc in next ch, repeat from * twice more—4 pats. Ch 2, turn.

Row 2: * Sk next hdc, 2 hdc in next hdc, repeat from * across. Ch 2, turn. Repeat row 2 for pat.

PANEL A (make 6): With W, ch 9 loosely. Work in pat 5 rows W. Break off W, leaving 10" end for sewing. Join MB, ch 2, turn. Always change colors this way. * Work in pat 5 rows MB, 5 rows W, repeat from * until 15 squares in all have been completed. End off.

PANEL B (make 3): With LB, ch 9. Work in pat 5 rows LB, * 5 rows MB, 15 rows LB, repeat from * twice, end 5 rows MB, 5 rows LB. End off.

PANEL C (make 2): With LB, ch 9. Work in pat 15 rows LB, * 5 rows MB, 15 rows LB, repeat from * twice. End off.

FINISHING: Beg with starting ch of each panel, sew panels tog, matching squares as follows: Sew tog panels (A, B, A, C) twice, (A, B, A) once.

FRINGE: Wind W yarn around a 2½" cardboard; cut at one end. Hold 3 strands tog; fold strands in half. With hook, draw folded lp through corner of one corner square, pull strand through lp and tighten. Knot 4 W fringe on each side edge of same corner square. Knot 4 matching fringe on edge of each square around entire edge of cover, working corner squares as before. Trim ends of fringe to 1½".

"Stained Glass" Afghan

The "stained glass" afghan is quick to crochet, using a giant-size hook and two strands of yarn. Five strips, each with six colors, are worked in afghan stitch and then joined together.

SIZE: 54″ x 62″.

MATERIALS: Knitting worsted or Orlon 4-ply knitting yarn, 8 oz. each of green (A), black (C), blue (E) and white (F); 10 oz. red (B); 6 oz. gold (D). Plastic crochet hook size Q.

GAUGE: Each strip (18 sts) = 10″; 9 rows = 7″.

AFGHAN: Note: Work with 2 strands of yarn throughout.

First Strip: With 2 strands of A, ch 18. Work in afghan stitch (see page 155), in following colors and rows: 8 rows A, 1 row C, 9 rows B, 1 row C, 4 rows D, 1 row C, 10 rows E, 1 row C, 6 rows A, 1 row C, 2 rows F, 1 row C, 16 rows B, 1 row C, 9 rows F, 1 row C and 6 rows E—78 rows. End off.

Slip-Stitch Edging: With C, make lp on hook. From right side, insert hook in hole next to first st of row 1, pull lp through to right side and through lp on hook, * insert hook next to first st in row above, pull lp through and through lp on hook, repeat from * to top of strip, sl st in each sp across top of strip, sl st in each sp down second side of strip, sl st in each sp across bottom of strip. End off.

Second Strip: With E, ch 18. Work in rows of afghan stitch as follows: 6 rows E, 1 row C, 4 rows D, 1 row C, 4 rows A, 1 row C, 4 rows E, 1 row C, 16 rows F, 1 row C, 8 rows B, 1 row C, 16 rows D, 1 row C, 10 rows A, 1 row C and 2 rows F—78 rows. Finish as for first strip. Sew second strip to first strip having starting chains at same edge.

Third Strip: With B, ch 18. Work in rows of afghan stitch as follows: 3 rows B, 1 row C, 8 rows F, 1 row C, 2 rows D, 1 row C, 15 rows B, 1 row C, 9 rows D, 1 row C, 11 rows A, 1 row C, 2 rows F, 1 row C and 21 rows E—78 rows. Finish as for first strip. Sew to second strip.

Fourth Strip: With F, ch 18. Work in rows of afghan stitch as follows: 3 rows F, 1 row C, 2 rows B, 1 row C, 5 rows E, 1 row C, 15 rows A, 1 row C, 8 rows F, 1 row C, 14 rows E, 1 row C, 9 rows B, 1 row C, 5 rows F, 1 row C and 9 rows D—78 rows. Finish as for first strip. Sew to third strip.

Fifth Strip: With A, ch 18. Work in rows of afghan stitch as follows: 11 rows A, 1 row C, 5 rows B, 1 row C, 5 rows F, 1 row C, 7 rows E, 1 row C, 3 rows D, 1 row C, 12 rows B, 1 row C, 6 rows F, 1 row C, 12 rows A, 1 row C and 9 rows B—78 rows. Finish as for first strip. Sew to fourth strip.

Edging: With 2 strands of C, make lp on hook. From right side, sc in corner st at one long edge; working through center of sl sts made on edge, sc in each st along edge. Sc around afghan in this manner, making 3 sc at each corner. Sl st in first sc; end off. Steam-press.

Leaf Cluster Afghan

A chevron-striped afghan in olive, tangerine, and gold is embossed with clusters of raised stitches resembling leaves. Three identical strips are crocheted and then sewn together for the afghan.

SIZE: About 54" x 63".

MATERIALS: Knitting worsted, 26 oz. olive green (O), 21 oz. each of tangerine (T) and gold (G). Aluminum crochet hook size K. Tapestry needle.

GAUGE: 3 sts = 1"; 12 rows = 5½".

Note: Afghan is made in three strips, each about 18" wide by 63" long. For longer afghan, add 12 rows to each strip.

STRIP (make 3): With O, ch 84. **Row 1:** Sc in 2nd ch from hook, sc in each of next 6 ch, * 3 sc in next ch, sc in each of next 7 ch, sk 2 ch, sc in each of next 7 ch, repeat from * 3 times, 3 sc in next ch, sc in each of next 7 ch. Ch 1, turn.

Row 2: Working in back lp of sts only throughout, sk first sc, sc in each of next 7 sc, * 3 sc in next sc (center st of 3 sc of last row), sc in each of next 7 sc, sk 2 sc, sc in each of next 7 sc, repeat from * 3 times, 3 sc in next sc, sc in each of next 6 sc, sk 1 sc, sc in last sc. Ch 1, turn.

Rows 3 and 4: Repeat row 2. At end of row 4, when making last sc, pull up a lp in last sc, drop O; attach T, complete sc with T. Ch 1, turn. Cut off O, leaving 8" end for sewing.

Row 5: With T, sk first sc, sc in back lp of each of next 3 sc, 1 dtr cluster around bar of 7th st of row 1 (st before center 3 sc forming point on 4th row below). **To**

make dtr cluster: * Yo hook 3 times, insert hook from right to left under st, pull up a lp, (yo hook and through 2 lps on hook) 3 times, repeat from * twice in same st—4 lps on hook; yo and through all 4 lps on hook—1 dtr cluster made. ** Sk 1 sc, sc in back lp of each of next 3 sc, 3 sc in back lp of center st, sc in back lp of each of next 3 sc, sk center 3 sc forming point of row 1, dtr cluster around bar of next st, sk 1 sc, sc in back lp of each of next 3 sc, sk 2 sc, sc in back lp of each of next 3 sc, dtr cluster in row 1 around bar of st before next center st, repeat from ** across, end with cluster, sk 1 sc, sc in back lp of each of next 2 sc, sk 1 sc, sc in back lp of last st. Ch 1, turn.

Rows 6-8: Repeat row 2. At end of row 8, complete last sc with G. Cut off T, leaving 8" end for sewing.

Rows 9-12: With G, repeat rows 5-8, working clusters in first T row. At end of row 12, complete last sc with O. Cut off G, leaving 8" end for sewing.

Repeat rows 5-8 for pattern, working clusters in first row of previous color, alternating stripes of O, T and G until strip measures 63", end with O stripe.

FINISHING: Threading yarn ends hanging at color changes in tapestry needle, weave strips tog from wrong side with matching colors, matching stripes. Steam-press on wrong side.

Motifs

Mohair Granny Squares Afghan

Favorite of all afghan motifs is the granny square, elaborated here in soft and fluffy mohair for an extra luxurious effect. The pattern can be used for granny afghans in knitting worsted or Orlon yarns of the same weight. More ounces of these yarns will be needed than the amounts of mohair.

SIZE: 50" x 65".

MATERIALS: Mohair or mohair-type yarn, 17 oz. of assorted colors, 7 oz. black. Crochet hook size G.

GAUGE: Each square = 7".

GRANNY SQUARE (make 63): With first color, ch 3, sl st in first ch to form ring.

Rnd 1: Ch 3 (counts as 1 dc), 2 dc in ring, (ch 3, 3 dc in ring) 3 times, ch 3, sl st in top of ch 3, sl st in each of next 2 dc, sl st in next ch. End off.

Rnd 2: Join another color in any ch-3 sp. Working over end of new color, ch 3, 2 dc in ch-3 sp, ch 3, 3 dc in same ch-3 sp, (ch 2; in next corner sp work 3 dc, ch 3, 3 dc) 3 times, ch 2, sl st in top of ch 3, sl st in each of next 2 dc, sl st in next ch. End off.

Rnd 3: Join another color in any ch-3 sp. Working over end of new color, ch 3, 2 dc in ch-3 sp, ch 3, 3 dc in same ch-3 sp, (ch 2, 3 dc in ch-2 sp, ch 2; in next corner sp work 3 dc, ch 3, 3 dc) 3 times, ch 2, 3 dc in next ch-2 sp, ch 2, sl st in top of ch 3, sl st in each of next 2 dc, sl st in next ch. End off.

Rnd 4: With another color, work as for rnd 3, working 2 groups of 3 dc on each side of square.

Rnd 5: With black, work as for rnd 3, working 3 groups of 3 dc on each side of square.

FINISHING: Overcast squares tog with black, sewing through back lps of sts. Make afghan 7 squares wide by 9 squares long.

BORDER: With black, work 1 rnd of dc around afghan, working dc in each dc and in each ch and working 3 dc, ch 3, 3 dc in each corner. Sl st in first dc. End off.

Baby Afghan

An appealing baby afghan is formed of fifteen blocks in five different arrangements of white, red, and shades of blue. Each block is made of granny squares at the center and corners of the solid single crochet sections. The border is a scalloped edge of shells.

SIZE: 34″ x 54″.

MATERIALS: Wintuk, 4-ply, 3 4-oz. skeins each of vermilion and white; 2 skeins Olympic blue; 1 skein each of electric blue and blue jewel; about 24 yards of pale gray-blue. Crochet hook size H.

GAUGE: 4 sc = 1″; 4 sc rows = 1″. Each square is 10″ square.

Note: Afghan is made of separate squares joined together. Squares are all worked in same manner, using different color arrangements.

SQUARE NO. 1 (make 4): **Center:** Beg at center with white, ch 4. Sl st in first ch to form ring.

Rnd 1 (right side): Ch 3, 2 dc in ring, ch 3, (3 dc in ring, ch 3) 3 times. Join with sl st to top of ch 3 at beg of rnd. End off.

Rnd 2: Join electric blue in any ch-3 sp, ch 3, 2 dc, ch 3, 3 dc in same sp, (ch 1, 3 dc, ch 3, 3 dc in next sp) 3 times, ch 1, sl st in top of ch 3. End off.

First Sc Section: Row 1: Join vermilion in any ch-3 sp, ch 1, sc in same sp, sc in each of next 3 dc, sc in next ch-1 sp, sc in each of next 3 dc, sc in next sp—9 sc. Ch 1, turn.

Row 2: Sc in each sc across. Ch 1, turn. Repeat row 2, 11 more times. End off.

2nd, 3rd and 4th Sc Sections: With right side facing, join vermilion in same ch-3 sp with last sc of row 1 of previous sc section, work as for first sc section.

Corner Motif (make 4): With vermilion, work as for center through rnd 1. With electric blue, work as for rnd 2.

Rnd 3: Join white in any ch-3 sp, ch 3, 2 dc in same sp, ch 3, 3 dc in same sp, * sk next dc, dc in each of next 2 dc, dc in ch-1 sp, dc in each of next 2 dc, sk next dc, 3 dc, ch 3, 3 dc in next ch-3 sp, repeat from * twice, sk next dc, dc in next 2 dc, dc in ch-1 sp, dc in next 2 dc. Sl st in top of ch 3. End off.

Join Corner Motifs: Place corner motifs in corner spaces of square. Baste 2 sides of each motif loosely to side edges of sc rows. Join Olympic blue to end of basting seam, ch 1. Working through both thicknesses, from right side, sl st in same place where yarn was joined, * ch 1, sl st loosely through next st on both pieces, repeat

from * along basted edges, matching inner corner of motif with corner sp of center. End off. Join other 3 motifs in same way.

Edging: From right side, join same color used for joining to any corner sp of square, ch 1, 3 sc in same sp, sc in each st and in each joining around, making 3 sc in each corner sp. End off.

SQUARE NO. 2 (make 4): Work as for Square No. 1, using colors as follows:

> **Rnd 1:** White.
> **Rnd 2:** Pale gray-blue.
> **Sc Sections:** Vermilion.
> **Corner Motifs: Rnd 1:** Blue jewel.
> **Rnd 2:** Vermilion.
> **Rnd 3:** White.
> **Joining and Edging:** Olympic blue.

SQUARE NO. 3 (make 4): Work as for Square No. 1, using colors as follows:

> **Rnd 1:** Vermilion.
> **Rnd 2:** Blue jewel.
> **Sc Sections:** White.
> **Corner Motifs: Rnd 1:** Electric blue.
> **Rnd 2:** Vermilion.
> **Rnd 3:** Blue jewel.
> **Joining and Edging:** Olympic blue.

SQUARE NO. 4 (make 2): Work as for Square No. 1, using colors as follows:

> **Rnd 1:** Pale gray-blue.
> **Rnd 2:** Vermilion.
> **Sc Sections:** White.
> **Corner Motifs: Rnd 1:** White.
> **Rnd 2:** Blue jewel.
> **Rnd 3:** Vermilion.
> **Joining and Edging:** Olympic blue.

SQUARE NO. 5 (make 1): Work as for Square No. 1, using colors as follows:

> **Rnd 1:** Vermilion.
> **Rnd 2:** White.
> **Sc Sections:** Blue jewel.
> **Corner Motifs: Rnd 1:** Olympic blue.
> **Rnd 2:** Blue jewel.
> **Rnd 3:** Vermilion.

Joining and Edging: Olympic blue.

Pin squares to measurement on a padded surface; cover with a damp cloth and allow to dry. Do not press.

TO JOIN SQUARES: Following chart for placement of squares, baste squares tog, matching sts and corners. Join 2 top rows tog with Olympic blue, working through both thicknesses as before, making sl st and ch 1 in each st across. Join bottom row to center row in same way. Join motifs across short rows in same way.

1	3	2	3	1
4	2	5	2	4
1	3	2	3	1

BORDER: Rnd 1: From right side, join Olympic blue in center sc of any corner 3-sc group, ch 1, 3 sc in same st, * sc evenly across squares, making 35 sc in each square, to next corner, 3 sc in corner st, repeat from * twice, sc evenly across last side. Sl st in first sc. Ch 1, turn.

Rnd 2: Sc in each sc around, 3 sc in each corner st. Sl st in first sc. End off. Turn.

Rnd 3: Join white to same sc as joining, ch 1, repeat rnd 2. Ch 1, turn.

Rnd 4: Repeat rnd 2. End off. Turn.

Rnd 5: Join vermilion to same sc as joining, ch 1, repeat rnd 2. Ch 1, turn.

Rnd 6: Repeat rnd 2. End off. Turn.

Rnd 7: From right side, join vermilion in center sc of any corner 3-sc group, ch 3, make 5 dc in same sc (shell), sk 2 sc, sc in next sc, * sk 2 sc, 6 dc in next sc (shell), sk 2 sc, sc in next sc, repeat from * around, skipping as necessary at corners to have a shell in each corner. Sl st in top of ch 3. End off.

Jewel Tone Afghan

This glorious afghan in jewel tones has granny-type squares of four sizes ingeniously placed and joined together with glowing striped borders. Add fringe of all colors to both ends.

SIZE: About 54″ x 80″, plus fringe.

MATERIALS: Knitting worsted or Orlon yarn of knitting-worsted weight, 4-oz. skeins: 2 skeins each of cerise, scarlet, dark purple, royal blue, and black; 1 skein each of magenta, light purple, teal blue, dark orange, light orange, light turquoise, dark turquoise, light violet, and dark yellow. Crochet hook size K.

GAUGE: 3 dc shell = 1″.

Notes: Join each rnd with a sl st in top of ch 3. Cut yarn, pull end through lp on hook. Join new color with sl st. Work over ends of previous color and new color to hide them.

AFGHAN: CENTER MOTIF: With cerise, ch 4, sl st in first ch to form ring.

Rnd 1: Ch 3 (counts as 1 dc), 11 dc in ring. Join; end off (see Notes).

Rnd 2: Join scarlet in sp between any 2 dc, ch 3, 2 dc in same sp, ch 1, 3 dc in same sp, * sk 3 dc, 3 dc, ch 1, 3 dc in next sp, repeat from * twice; join; end off.

Rnd 3: Join magenta in ch-1 corner sp, ch 3, 2 dc in same sp, 3 dc in next sp between shells of 3 dc, * 3 dc, ch 1, 3 dc in next corner ch-1 sp, 3 dc in next sp between shells, repeat from * twice, 3 dc in first corner sp, ch 1; join; end off.

Rnd 4: Join light purple in ch-1 corner sp, ch 3, 2 dc in same sp, (3 dc in next sp) twice, * 3 dc, ch 1, 3 dc in next corner ch-1 sp, (3 dc in next sp) twice, repeat from * twice, 3 dc in first corner sp, ch 1; join; end off.

Rnds 5-12: Work as for rnd 4, using dark purple, royal blue, teal blue, black, dark orange, light orange, cerise, and scarlet in order, having 1 extra shell on each side each rnd.

SMALL MOTIF: With dark turquoise, royal blue, dark purple, and cerise, work rnds 1-4 of center motif. Make 8 small motifs the same.

With light purple, dark turquoise, black, and dark purple, work 8 small motifs the same.

Joining: Place small motifs around center motif, alternating colors, having cerise-edged motifs at corners. With loose sc, from wrong side, join small motifs tog, and join small motifs to center motif, using colors to match one edge to be joined.

STRIPED BORDER: Rnd 1: Join black in any corner sp of large block just made. Ch 3, 2 dc in same sp, * dc in next sp between dc's, repeat from * around, making 3 dc in each corner; join to top of ch 3; end off.

Rnd 2: Join light turquoise in sp between any 2 dc, ch 3, * dc in next sp, repeat from * around, making 2 dc in each of 2 sps at corners; join; end off.

Rnd 3: Join royal blue in sp between any 2 dc, ch 3, * dc in next sp, repeat from * around, making 3 dc in each corner; join; end off.

Rnd 4: With light violet, repeat rnd 2.

Rnd 5: With light purple, repeat rnd 3.

MEDIUM MOTIF: With dark yellow, dark orange, light orange, cerise, and scarlet, work rnds 1-5 of center motif. Make 12 medium motifs the same.

With cerise, scarlet, magenta, light purple, and dark purple, work 12 medium motifs the same.

Joining: Place medium motifs around striped border, alternating colors, having scarlet-edged motifs at corners. Join motifs tog and join motifs to striped border with sc.

STRIPED BORDER: Rnd 1: Join black in any sp between 2 dc. Ch 3, * dc in next sp, repeat from * to sp before first corner shell, sk first corner shell, make 3 dc, ch 1, 3 dc in corner, sk 2nd corner shell, repeat from first * around. Join; end off.

Rnds 2-5: Repeat rnd 1 with scarlet, dark purple, royal blue, and teal blue.

END MOTIF: With black, teal blue, dark purple, light turquoise, royal blue, and light violet, work rnds 1-6 of center motif. Make 8 motifs the same.

With light turquoise, teal blue, dark turquoise, dark purple, black, and royal blue, make 6 motifs the same.

Joining: Place 7 motifs across each end of afghan, alternating colors. Join motifs tog and to striped border with sc.

END BORDER: Row 1: From right side, join dark purple in corner sp at top edge of afghan; ch 3, dc in each sp between dc's across top edge. End off.

Row 2: Join scarlet in sp between ch 3 and first dc of row 1, ch 3, dc in each sp between dc's across. End off.

Row 3: With cerise, work as for row 2.

Make same border at bottom of afghan.

FINISHING: Join black in any sp between 2 dc on edge. Ch 3, * dc in next sp, repeat from * around, working 3 dc in each corner of afghan.

Run in all yarn ends. Steam-press afghan lightly.

FRINGE: Wind yarns of all colors around cardboard or book 9″ long. Cut at one end. Using 3 strands tog, fold strands in half, pull folded ends through sp at one end of afghan, pull 6 ends through loop; tighten knot. Knot 6 ends tog below first knot. Knot fringe in every other sp along top and bottom of afghan.

Color Wheels Afghan

Color wheels offer you a great way to use up odds and ends of knitting worsted. Make strips in slipper stitch crochet using five colors repeated once. Form strips into wheels, gathering in the center with black, then work around the outer edges of the wheels, shaping into squares.

SIZE: 50″ x 70″.

MATERIALS: Knitting worsted, about 42 oz. of assorted colors and 10 4-oz. skeins of black (background color). For a color scheme of 5 colors, plus background color, 3 4-oz. skeins of first color, 2 skeins each of 4 other colors and 10 4-oz. skeins of background color are needed. Crochet hook size G or 6.

GAUGE: Each square = 10″.

Note: If leftover yarns are used, use a different color for each section of wheel, having as many colors as desired. Make squares either all the same or in different arrangements of colors. Always have same background color for all squares. If five colors only are used for wheels, make all squares in the same color arrangement.

AFGHAN: SQUARE (make 35): **Center Section** (center section is worked in rows into a straight strip about 17″ long, then gathered into a round shape):

Row 1: With first color, ch 11. Sc in 2nd ch from hook, sc in each remaining 9 ch. Ch 1, turn.

Row 2: Working in back lp only of each st, sc in each of 10 sc. Ch 1, turn.

Rows 3-6: Repeat row 2. End off. This completes first section. Turn.

Row 7: Join 2nd color with sc in back lp of first sc, sc in back lp of each remaining 9 sc. Ch 1, turn.

Rows 8-12: Repeat row 2. End off.

Rows 13-18: With 3rd color, repeat rows 7-12.

Rows 19-24: With 4th color, repeat rows 7-12.

Rows 25-30: With 5th color, repeat rows 7-12. Repeating 5 colors in same order or using a different color for each section, work 5 more 6-row sections in same way—10 sections; 60 rows.

CENTER RING: Rnd 1: With background color, join yarn with sl st in end sc of row 1 of center section. Ch 3; working tightly over end of rows, work a 3-dc cluster over first section as follows: yo hook, draw up a lp in same end st as sl st, yo and through 2 lps, (yo hook, sk next row, draw up a lp in end sc of next row, yo and through 2 lps) twice, yo and through all 4 lps on hook (3-dc cluster made), * sk next row (last row of section), work a 3-dc cluster in next section, repeat from * across, end sl st in top of first 3-dc cluster—10 clusters.

Rnd 2: (Sk next cluster, sl st in next cluster) 5 times. End off.

With first color, overcast last row of strip to ch at beg of strip.

OUTER SECTION: Rnd 1: Working around outer edge of center section, join background color with sc in end sc of row 1, * 2 sc in end st of next row, sc in end st of next row, repeat from * around, end 2 sc in end st of last row, sl st in first sc at beg of rnd—90 sc.

Rnd 2: Ch 1, sc in same sc as sl st, sc in each of next 7 sc, * 2 sc in next sc, sc in each of next 8 sc, repeat from * around, end with 2 sc in last sc, sl st in first sc—100 sc.

Rnd 3: Ch 1, sc in same sc as sl st, sc in each of next 9 sc, * ch 1, sk next sc, 2-dc cluster in next sc (to make 2-dc cluster, yo hook, draw up a lp in next sc, yo and through 2 lps, yo hook, draw up a lp in same sc, yo and through 2 lps, yo and through all 3 lps on hook), ch 1, sk next sc, work a 2-tr cluster in next sc (to make 2-tr cluster: holding back on hook last lp of each tr, make 2 tr in next sc, yo and through all 3 lps on hook), ch 1, sk next sc, work a 2-dtr cluster in next sc (work as for 2-tr cluster, but yo hook 3 times for each dtr), ch 1, sk next sc, work a 2-tr tr cluster in next sc (yo hook 4 times), ch 5, 2-tr tr cluster in same sc as last cluster, ch 1, sk next sc, 2-dtr cluster in next sc, ch 1, sk next sc, 2-tr cluster in next sc, ch 1, sk next sc, 2-dc cluster in next sc, ch 1, sk next sc, sc in each of next 10 sc, repeat from * around, end last repeat with ch 1, sk last sc, sl st in first sc. End off.

Rnd 4: With first color, join yarn with sc in same sc as last sl st, sc in each of next 9 sc, * (sc in next ch-1 sp, sc in next cluster) 4 times, 5 sc in corner ch-5 sp, (sc in next cluster, sc in next ch-1 sp) 4 times, sc in each of next 10 sc, repeat from * around, end last repeat with sl st in first sc. End off.

Rnd 5: Join background color with sc in same sc as last sl st, * sc in each sc to center st of next 5-sc group at corner, 3 sc in center st, repeat from * around, end sc in each remaining sc, sl st in first sc. End off.

FINISHING: Pin out each square to correct size on padded surface; cover with a damp cloth; steam with a warm iron but do not press. Let dry.

With background color, overcast squares tog from corner st to corner st, matching sts. Join squares in 5 rows of 7 squares each, then sew rows tog.

Border: Join background color with sc in center sc at corner of afghan; 2 more sc in same st, * sc in each sc to center st at next corner, 3 sc in corner st, repeat from * around, end sl st in first sc.

Rnd 2: See Note below. Sl st in next sc, ch 1, 3 sc in same sc as sl st, * sc in each sc to center st at next corner, 3 sc in corner sc, repeat from * around, end sl st in first sc.

Rnd 3: Repeat rnd 2. End off.

Note: If desired, rnd 2 may be worked in first color.

Star Mosaic Afghan

White stars on a field of brilliant blue make a dazzling afghan design. The six-sided motifs are crocheted with star-puff centers, edged with blue, and joined together in the crocheting to form a tilelike pattern. For a finishing touch, add white tassels to top and bottom edges.

SIZE: 48″ x 63″, plus tassels.

MATERIALS: Sweater and afghan yarn, 9 2-oz. skeins of white (A) and 12 skeins of blue (B). Crochet hook size H.

GAUGE: One motif = 2¾″ from one side to opposite side.

FIRST MOTIF: With A, ch 4, sl st in first ch to form ring.

Rnd 1: Ch 3, * (yo hook, insert hook in ring and draw up a ¾″ lp) 4 times, yo hook and through all 9 lps on hook, ch 1 to fasten; ch 4, repeat from * 5 times, insert hook in ch 1 at top of first cluster, draw through a lp, cut A; draw B through 2 lps on hook.

Rnd 2: With B, sl st in ch-4 sp, ch 3 (counts as 1 dc); working over ends of A and B, make 4 dc in ch-4 sp, * ch 3, 5 dc in next ch-4 sp, repeat from * 4 times, ch 3, sl st in top of starting ch. End off.

SECOND MOTIF: Rnd 1: Work as for first motif.

Rnd 2: With B, sl st in ch-4 sp, ch 3, 4 dc in ch-4 sp, ch 1; holding first motif in back of work, wrong sides tog, sl st in any ch-3 sp of first motif, ch 1, 5 dc in next ch-4 sp, ch 1, sl st in next ch-3 sp of first motif, ch 1, 5 dc in next ch-4 sp, ch 3, work to end of rnd as for first motif.

FIRST ROW: Work 15 more motifs, joining to preceding motif as for second motif—17 motifs.

SECOND ROW: FIRST MOTIF: Work as for first motif through rnd 1.

Rnd 2: With B, sl st in ch-4 sp, ch 3, 4 dc in ch-4 sp, ch 1; holding first motif of first row in back of work, wrong sides tog, join to ch-3 sp before joining of first two motifs of first row, ch 1, 5 dc in next ch-4 sp, ch 1, join in sl st joining first and second motifs of first row, ch 1, 5 dc in next ch-4 sp, ch 1, join to next ch-3 sp of second motif of first row, ch 1, work to end of rnd as for first motif.

Work second motif, joining to first free sp of first motif, to next joining st (between first motif of second row and second motif of first row), to next joining st (between second and third motifs of first row), finish motif as before. Continue in this manner, joining 16 motifs of second row to 17 motifs of first row.

Alternating rows of 17 motifs with rows of 16 motifs, work until there are 14 rows of 17 motifs and 13 rows of 16 motifs.

FINISHING: With B, sc around afghan, making 1 sc in each dc and 1 sc in each sp. Join to first sc. End off.

If desired, steam-press afghan, using a steam iron or a damp cloth and a dry iron.

Tassels (make 34): Wind A 10 times around a 2¼″ cardboard. Tie strands tog at one edge of cardboard; cut strands at opposite edge. Wind a separate strand of A several times around all strands ¼″ below top of tassel. Hide ends inside tassel. Tie a tassel to each free ch-3 sp across top and bottom of afghan; hide ends inside tassels. Trim tassels evenly.

Pansy Afghan

Rows of blue and yellow pansies with smiling faces make a cheery and unusual afghan. Fluted pansy motifs are made separately and joined where their petals touch. The spaces between the motifs are filled in lightly for a lacy effect.

SIZE: 48″ x 66″.

MATERIALS: Knitting worsted, 5 4-oz. skeins black, 3 skeins each of peacock and royal blue, 2 skeins each of yellow and orange. Crochet hook size I.

GAUGE: Each pansy approx. 6″.

AFGHAN: Blue Pansy: With black, ch 7, sl st in first ch to form ring. **Rnd 1:** Ch 2 (counts as 1 dc), 14 dc in ring. Sl st in top of ch 2—15 dc. End off.

Rnd 2: Join yellow in any dc, ch 3, dc in each of next 2 dc, (ch 7, dc in each of next 3 dc) 4 times, end ch 7, sl st in top of ch 3—5 ch-7 lps. End off.

Rnd 3: Join peacock in center dc of any 3-dc group; (15 dc over next ch-7 lp, sl st in center dc of next 3-dc group) 3 times. End off. Join royal blue in same st with end of peacock, ch 4; in next ch-7 lp make (dtr, ch 1) 12 times, (tr, ch 1) twice, and (dc, ch 1) twice; sc in center dc of 3-dc group, (ch 1, dc) twice, (ch 1, tr) twice, and (ch 1, dtr) 12 times in last ch-7 lp. Ch 4, sl st in same st with peacock. End off.

Rnd 4: Join black with sc in peacock joining st at beg of rnd 3, (ch 1, sc in next st) across 3 peacock petals, sc in ch-4 lp of royal blue, ch 3, sc in same lp, (ch 3, sc in next ch-1 sp) across 2 royal blue petals, end ch 3, sc in ch-4 lp, sl st in first sc; end off. Weave in yarn end on wrong side.

Yellow Pansy: Work as for blue pansy, working rnd 1 in yellow, rnd 2 in black, rnd 3 with 3 yellow petals and 2 orange petals, and rnd 4 with black.

TO JOIN PANSIES: See diagram. Pansies are joined on rnd 4 with sl st in corresponding ch-1 or ch-3 lp of previous pansy. Diagram shows points of joining.

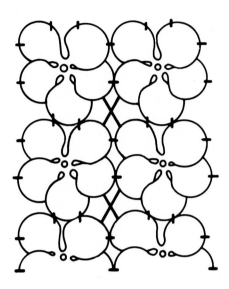

Make 59 blue pansies and 29 yellow pansies, joining them in the arrangement shown in chart.

Fill-in Motif: Fill in space between 4 motifs as follows: With black, make lp on hook, work dtr in edge of petal on each of 4 motifs (see large X on diagram). Sl st in first dtr. End off. Weave in ends.

B	B	B	B	B	B	B	B
B	B	B	B	B	B	Y	B
B	B	B	B	B	Y	B	B
B	B	B	B	Y	Y	Y	B
B	B	B	Y	Y	Y	B	B
B	B	Y	B	Y	Y	Y	B
B	B	B	Y	Y	B	B	B
B	B	Y	B	Y	Y	B	B
B	Y	B	Y	B	Y	B	B
B	Y	Y	Y	Y	B	B	B
Y	B	Y	Y	Y	Y	B	B

Bright Squares Afghan

Easy-to-make squares, all the same except for their colors, are arranged in a bold, attractive step pattern.

SIZE: 44″ x 60″.

MATERIALS: Knitting worsted-weight yarn, 2 4-oz. skeins sun gold (A), cyclamen (B), Persian blue (C), orange (D), white (E), and royal blue (F). Crochet hook size G.

GAUGE: Each square = 4¼″.

MOTIF (make 30 A, 22 each of B, C, D, E, and F): Beg at center, ch 3, sl st in first ch to form ring.

Rnd 1: Ch 3, 11 dc in ring. Sl st in top of ch 3.

Rnd 2: Ch 3 (counts as 1 dc), dc in same place as sl st, (2 dc in next dc) twice * ch 1 (corner), 2 dc in each of next 3 dc, repeat from * twice, ch 1, sl st in top of ch 3.

Rnd 3: Sl st in next dc, ch 3, 2 dc in same dc, * (sk 1 dc, 3 dc in next dc) twice, ch 3 for corner, sk corner sp and next dc, 3 dc in next dc, repeat from * around, end ch 3 for last corner, sl st in top of ch 3 at beg of rnd.

Rnd 4: Ch 1, sc around, working sc in each of 9 dc on each side, 3 sc in each corner sp. Sl st in first sc. End off.

FINISHING: Sew squares tog through back lps of sts, arranging squares as shown on chart.

A	A	A	A	A	A	A	A	A	A	A
A	A	A	A	A	A	A	A	A	B	B
A	A	A	A	A	B	B	B	B	B	C
A	A	A	A	B	B	B	B	C	C	C
A	A	A	B	B	B	C	C	C	D	
B	B	B	B	B	C	C	D	D	D	
B	B	B	B	C	C	C	D	D	E	
C	C	C	C	C	C	D	D	E	E	
C	C	C	C	C	D	D	E	E	F	
D	D	D	D	D	D	E	E	F	F	
D	D	D	D	D	D	E	F	F	F	
E	E	E	E	E	E	E	F	F	F	
E	E	E	E	E	E	E	F	F	F	
F	F	F	F	F	F	F	F	F	F	

Gold-Edged Squares Afghan

Simplest of all granny squares is this giant two-color motif, worked all in white, then edged on the final round with contrasting gold yarn. The squares are sewn together, then the afghan is edged and fringed with gold.

SIZE: 44"x 66", plus fringe.

MATERIALS: Knitting worsted-weight yarn, 6 4-oz. skeins white, 2 skeins gold. Crochet hook size H. Tapestry needle.

GAUGE: Each square = 10½".

SQUARE (make 24): Beg at center, with white, ch 3, sl st in first ch to form ring.

Rnd 1: Ch 3 (counts as first dc), 2 dc in ring, (ch 3, 3 dc in ring) 3 times, ch 3, sl st in top of ch 3 at beg of rnd, sl st in each of next 2 dc, sl st in first ch-3 sp.

Rnd 2: Ch 3, 2 dc in ch-3 sp, ch 3, 3 dc in same ch-3 sp, (ch 2, 3 dc, ch 3, 3 dc in next ch-3 sp) 3 times, ch 2, sl st in top of ch 3 at beg of rnd, sl st in each of next 2 dc, sl st in corner ch-3 sp.

Rnd 3: Ch 3, 2 dc in corner sp, ch 3, 3 dc in same sp, (ch 2, 3 dc in next sp, ch 2, 3 dc, ch 3, 3 dc in next corner sp) 3 times, ch 2, 3 dc in next sp, ch 2, sl st in top of ch 3 at beg of rnd, sl st in each of next 2 dc, sl st in corner ch-3 sp.

Rnd 4: Ch 3, 2 dc in corner sp, ch 3, 3 dc in same sp, * (ch 2, 3 dc in next sp) twice, ch 2, 3 dc, ch 3, 3 dc in next corner sp, repeat from * twice, (ch 2, 3 dc in next sp) twice, ch 2, sl st in top of ch 3 at beg of rnd, sl st in each of next 2 dc, sl st in corner ch-3 sp.

Rnds 5-7: Work as for rnd 4, having 3 groups of 3 dc between corners on rnd 5, 4 groups on rnd 6, and 5 groups on rnd 7. End off.

Rnd 8: With gold, work as for rnd 4, having 6 groups of 3 dc between corners. End off.

FINISHING: With gold, sew squares tog, sewing through back lps of sts only, having 6 rows of squares 4 squares wide.

Edging: With gold, work in 3 dc, ch-2 pat around entire afghan.

FRINGE: Cut gold strands 12" long. Holding 5 strands together, knot a fringe in each space across bottom and top edges of afghan.

Dusty Rose Afghan

An unusual arrangement of oblong motifs in three tones of dusty rose adds interest to this easy-to-crochet afghan. After the pieces are sewn together, the resulting open squares are filled in with dark rose.

SIZE: 50″ x 64″.

MATERIALS: Knitting worsted-weight yarn, 3 4-oz. skeins each of light tone (A), and medium tone (B), and 5 skeins dark tone (C). Crochet hook size I. Tapestry needle.

GAUGE: Each motif = 3½″ x 7″.

MOTIF (make 99): With A, ch 17.

Rnd 1: Dc in 5th ch from hook, ch 2; in same ch make dc, ch 1, dc (group st), (ch 1, sk 2 ch, group st in next ch) 4 times, (ch 2, group st in same ch as last group st) twice; working along opposite side of starting ch (ch 1, sk 2 ch, group st in next ch) 4 times, ch 2, sl st in 3rd ch of starting ch 4. End off.

Rnd 2: Join B with sl st in ch-2 sp before joining of rnd 1, ch 4 (counts as 1 dc and ch 1), dc in same sp, ch 3, group st in same corner sp, ch 2, group st, ch 3, group st in next corner sp, (ch 1, group st in next sp between group sts) 4 times, ch 1, group st, ch 3, group st in next corner sp, ch 2, group st, ch 3, group st in next corner sp, (ch 1, group st in next sp between group sts) 4 times, ch 1, sl st in 3rd ch of ch 4. End off.

Rnd 3: Join C with sl st in corner ch-3 sp after joining, ch 4, dc in same sp, ch 3, group st in same corner sp, * ch 1, group st in sp between corners, ch 1, group st, ch 3, group st in next corner, (ch 1, group st in next sp between group sts) 5 times, ch 1, group st, ch 3, group st in corner sp, ch 1, group st in sp between corners, ch 1, group st, ch 3, group st in next corner, (ch 1, group st in next sp between group sts) 5 times, ch 1, sl st in 3rd ch of ch 4. End off.

FINISHING: Pin 2 motifs tog, placing the 3 group sts at end of first motif opposite the 3 center group sts on long side of 2nd motif. With C in yarn needle, join yarn in center ch at corner of first motif, join to center of first group st on side of 2nd motif. Sew motifs tog through back lps of sts only, ending with center ch at next corner of first motif joined to center of 5th group st on side of 2nd motif. Following chart for arrangement of motifs, sew all motifs tog in this way, having afghan 9 motifs wide, as shown on chart, and 11 rows long.

Fill-In Motif: In the space left between 4 motifs, work fill-in motif as follows: with lp of C on hook, dc in any corner ch-3 sp, (dc in ch-1 sp between group sts on next motif, dc in corner ch-3 sp of same motif) 3 times, dc in ch-1 sp between group sts on next motif, sl st in top of first dc. End off.

Edging: Join A in ch-3 sp at lower right-hand corner of afghan, work sc, ch 3, sc in corner sp. Working up side of afghan, (ch 1, sc in ch-1 sp of next group st, ch 1, sc in ch-1 sp between group sts) 6 times, ch 1, sc in ch-1 sp of next group st, ch 1, sc in corner sp of same motif, sc in seam, sc in ch-1 sp of next group st, (ch 1, sc in next ch-1 sp) twice, ch 1, sc in next corner ch-3 sp, (ch 1, sc in next ch-1 sp) 5 times, ch 1, sc, ch 3, sc in next corner ch-3 sp; continue around in this manner, working sc, ch 3, sc in each outer corner ch-3 sp, and 3 sc tog in each inner corner between motifs. Join. End off.

FRINGE: Cut strands of A 14″ long. Holding 6 strands tog, knot 3 fringes in lower edge of 5 vertical motifs at bottom of afghan. Repeat on upper edge of afghan.

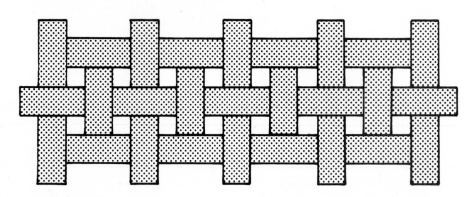

Colonial Afghan

Large red-and-white motifs, 9″ in diameter, are made in double crochet, with reverse single crochet forming raised ridges around circular bands. Early American in mood, the afghan is enhanced by fat red tassels at the sides.

Chart indicates how to assemble large and small motifs for Colonial Afghan.

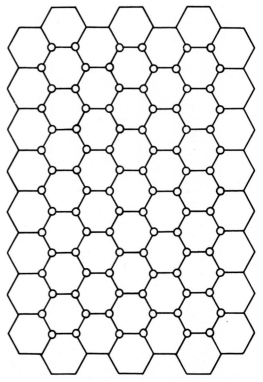

SIZE: 56″ x 81″.

MATERIALS: Yarn of knitting-worsted weight, 4-ply, 36 2-oz. balls white (A); 18 balls scarlet (B). Aluminum crochet hook size G.

GAUGE: Large motif = 9″ diameter.

LARGE MOTIF (make 59): Beg at center with A and size G crochet hook, ch 7, sl st in first ch to form ring.

Rnd 1: Ch 3 (counts as 1 dc), 19 dc in ring. Join with sl st in top of ch 3.

Rnd 2: Ch 1, sc in each dc around. Sl st in first sc of rnd.

Rnd 3: 2 dc (ch 3 for first dc) in each sc around—40 dc. Sl st in front lp of first dc.

Rnd 4: Working from left to right, work a reverse sc in front lp of each dc around. (To work a reverse sc, turn hook to upright position with hook down; insert hook from front to back through front lp of st; catch yarn and bring through st, yo and through 2 lps on hook.) Join with sl st in first st. End off; do not turn.

Rnd 5: With B, make lp on hook, working in back lp of dc on rnd 3, * work 2 dc in next dc, dc in each of next 3 dc, repeat from * around—50 dc. Sl st in first dc.

Rnd 6: Ch 3, * 2 dc in next dc, dc in each of next 4 dc, repeat from * around—60 dc. Sl st in top of ch 3.

Rnd 7: Repeat rnd 4. End off.

Rnd 8: With A, make lp on hook, working in back lp of dc on rnd 6, * work 2 dc in first dc, dc in each of next 5 dc, repeat from * around—70 dc. Sl st in first dc.

Rnd 9: Ch 3, * 2 dc in next dc, dc in each of next 6 dc, repeat from * around—80 dc. Sl st in top of ch 3.

Rnd 10: Repeat rnd 4. End off.

Rnd 11: With B, make lp on hook, working in back lp of dc on rnd 9, * work 2 dc in next dc, dc in each of next 4 dc, repeat from * around—96 dc. Sl st in first dc.

Rnd 12: Ch 3, * 2 dc in next dc, dc in each of next 7 dc, repeat from * around—108 dc. Sl st in top of ch 3.

Rnd 13: Repeat rnd 4. End off.

Rnd 14: With A, make lp on hook, working in back lp of dc on rnd 12, * work 2 dc in first dc, dc in each of next 8 dc, repeat from * around—120 dc. Sl st in first dc.

Rnd 15: Ch 3, * 2 dc in next dc, dc in each of next 9 dc, repeat from * around—132 dc. Sl st in top of ch 3.

Rnd 16: Repeat rnd 4. End off.

JOINING: See chart. From wrong side, sew large motifs tog with overcast stitch, joining 16 sts of each motif to 16 sts of another motif. At each of six "corners," skip 6 sts to allow for insertion of small motifs. At scalloped edges of afghan, where no small motifs are to be inserted, sew only 12 sts tog. If desired, crochet motifs tog with sl st, using a finer hook.

SMALL MOTIFS (make 90): Beg at center with A and size G hook, ch 7, sl st in first ch to form ring.

Rnd 1: Ch 3, 17 dc in ring. Join with a sl st in top of ch 3. Turn.

From wrong side, place small motif into space between large motifs; join with sc to 18 free sts on large motifs. End off.

Run in all ends on wrong side.

Tassels (make 30): Wind B 42 times around 3½″ cardboard. Tie one end; cut other edge. Wind B around tassel ½″ below tied end. Attach to sides of afghan as pictured.

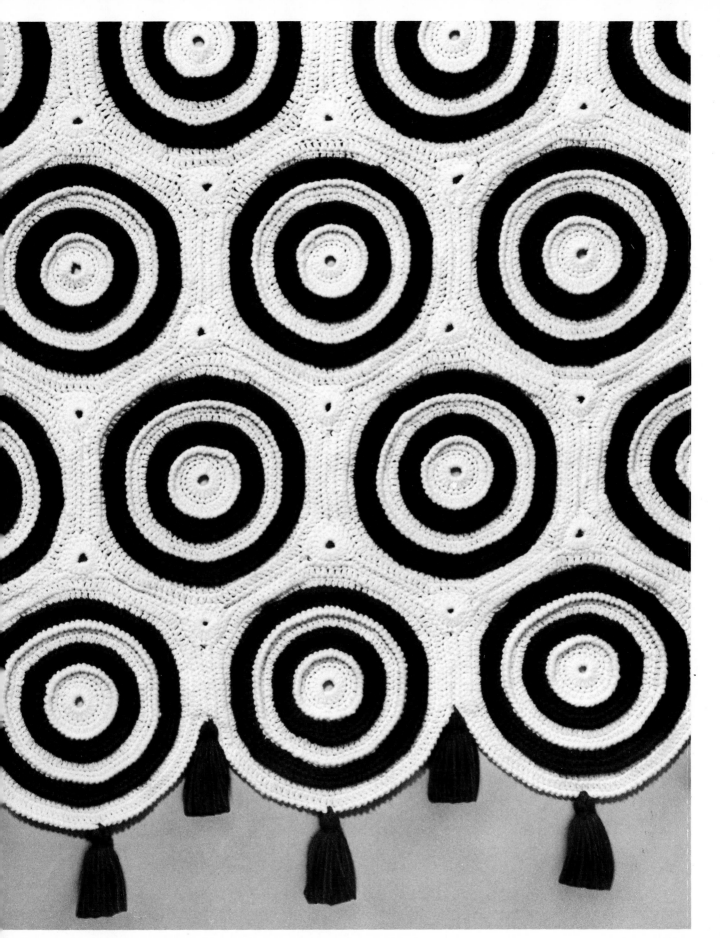

Two-Tone Checkerboard Afghan and Pillow

A two-tone afghan of square motifs in a checkerboard arrangement is at home in any surroundings. The motifs are crocheted in one tone and decorated with raised ridges of the contrasting color. Directions are also given for a little throw pillow with the same square motif.

SIZE: Afghan, about 52″ x 65″; pillow, 8″ square.

MATERIALS: Knitting worsted, 6 4-oz. skeins color A, 6 skeins color B, for afghan and one pillow. Plastic crochet hook size 6 or H. Tapestry needle. Foam rubber, 2″ thick, 8″ square, or 2 squares, 1″ thick. Cotton fabric ¼ yard.

GAUGE: 3 tr = 1″. Each square measures 7″.

Afghan:

Note: Work in back lp of each tr throughout.

FIRST SQUARE (make 32): Starting at center, with A, ch 5. Join with sl st to form ring. **Rnd 1:** Ch 4, 3 tr in ring, * ch 3, 4 tr in ring, repeat from * twice, ch 3, join with sl st to top of ch 4.

Rnd 2: Ch 4, tr in next 3 tr, * in corner sp, work 2 tr, ch 3 and 2 tr, tr in next 4 tr, repeat from * around, end with 2 tr, ch 3, 2 tr in corner sp, join to top of ch 4.

Rnd 3: Ch 4, tr in next 5 tr, * in corner sp, work 2 tr, ch 3 and 2 tr, tr in next 8 tr, repeat from * around, end with tr in 2 tr, join to top of ch 4.

Rnd 4: Ch 4, tr in next 7 tr, * in corner sp, work 2 tr, ch 3 and 2 tr, tr in next 12 tr, repeat from * around, end with tr in 4 tr, join. Break off.

Trimming: Attach B to any corner at top of rnd 1, sc in same place, work sc between tr's at corners, work sc in front lp of each tr of rnd 1. Join and break off. Work sc ridge in same manner at top of rnds 2 and 3.

SECOND SQUARE (make 31): Work same as first square, reversing colors.

FINISHING: Arrange squares 7 across and 9 in length, alternating colors and having a first square in each corner. Thread tapestry needle with A or B, sew squares tog with overcast st, picking up 1 lp only in top of each st of rnd 4. With A, work 2 rows sc all around afghan, working in both lps of each st and making 3 sc in each corner.

Pillow:

Make one piece same as first square, one same as second square.

Boxing Strip: With A, ch 10. **Row 1:** Dc in 4th ch from hook and in each ch across—8 dc, counting ch 3 as 1 dc. Ch 3, turn.

Row 2: Sk first dc, dc in each st across, dc in top of ch 3. Ch 3, turn. Repeat row 2 until strip is long enough to fit around four sides of pillow. Break off. Sew ends of boxing strip tog.

Cover foam rubber 8″ square x 2″ thick with fabric. Place one square on each side of pillow and, using A, sc squares to boxing strip.

Butterfly Squares Afghan

Bright butterflies are crocheted right into the background of these double crochet squares. Butterfly motifs are then edged round with filet crochet. Picture (page 66) courtesy of Bucilla Needlecraft.

SIZE: About 49″ x 66″.

MATERIALS: Sport yarn, 5 2-oz. skeins (about 225 yards per skein) of periwinkle blue (A); 9 skeins grape punch (B); 2 skeins cyclamen (C); and 1 skein white (D). Crochet hook size E.

GAUGE: 5 dc = 1″; 3 rows = 1″.

AFGHAN: SQUARE (make 12): **Center:** With A, ch 44.

Row 1 (wrong side): Dc in 4th ch from hook (counts as 2 dc) and in each remaining ch—42 dc. Turn each row.

Row 2: Sl st in first st, ch 3 (counts as 1 dc), dc in next st and in each dc across, end dc in top of ch 3—42 dc.

Row 3: Repeat row 2. Leaving an end of about 10 yards, cut yarn. Wind this end around a small bobbin. Wind another small bobbin with about 10 yards of A. Cut a few strands of A, B, C, and D in lengths of about 1 yard. Cut more as needed.

TO CHANGE COLORS OR ADD NEW STRANDS: Draw lp of new color or strand through last 2 lps, completing last dc of previous color. Always draw new and dropped colors just tightly enough to keep work flat and elastic. Drop colors or strands not in use to wrong side of work. For neatness on wrong side, where necessary, work over strand of previous color used or strand from row below, so that it will be in proper working position for use on next row without having to be carried across surface of wrong side.

Row 4 (right side): Working from chart, with A work 12 dc, joining a B strand by drawing it through last 2 lps of last A dc, drop A to wrong side; work 6 B dc, joining a new A strand in last B dc; 2 A dc over last B strand, drop B; 4 more A dc, joining a new B strand in last A dc, drop A; 6 B dc joining bobbin of A in last B dc, 2 A dc over last B strand, drop B; 12 A dc.

Row 5 (wrong side): With A, work 10 dc, changing to B by picking up B strand from row below and drawing it through last 2 lps of last A st, drop A to wrong side; 2 B dc, joining a C strand in last B dc, drop B; 6 C dc, joining a

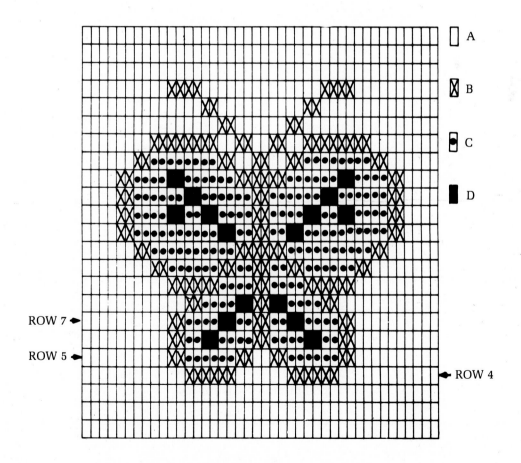

ROW 7 ➤

ROW 5 ➤

➤ ROW 4

A
B
C
D

new B strand in last C dc, 2 B dc over C and A strands from row below, changing to this A strand, drop B and C; 2 A dc, changing to B strand from row below, break A; 2 B dc, joining a new C strand, drop B; 6 C dc, joining a new B strand, drop C; 2 B dc over A strand from row below, changing to this A strand, drop B; 10 A dc.

Row 6: With A, work 10 dc, change to B, drop A; 2 B dc, change to C, drop B; 2 C dc, joining a D strand, 2 D dc over C, 2 C dc over D, drop D, 2 more C dc over B strand from row below, change to this B strand, drop C; 2 B dc, change to C, drop B; 4 C dc, joining a new D strand, 2 D dc over C, drop D, 2 C dc, change to B, drop C, 2 B dc, change to A, drop B; 10 A dc.

Beg with row 7, follow chart adding new strands and working over strands as necessary, until 23 rows have been completed, end on wrong side. Do not break yarn.

BORDER: Rnd 1: Ch 4, turn, dc in 2nd st, * ch 1, sk 1 st, dc in next st, repeat from * 18 times, ch 1, dc in sp under ch 3 at end of row; ch 3, dc in same sp for corner, sk base of last row of square, ** ch 1, dc in base of end dc of next row, repeat from ** 19 times ending with last dc in base of 2nd row from end, ch 1, dc in sp under end st of last row of square, ch 3, dc in same sp for corner; ch 1, dc in next st, continue around, working lower and right side edges to correspond to opposite edges, end with ch 3, join with sl st in 3rd ch of ch 4 at beg of rnd—21 sps on each side, plus 4 corner sps.

Rnd 2: Turn, sl st into corner sp, ch 3, turn, dc in same sp for half of corner, * dc in each dc and in each sp to within next corner, 2 dc, ch 3, 2 dc all in corner sp, repeat from * around, end with dc in last dc, 2 dc in corner, ch 3, join with sl st in top of ch 3 at beg of rnd to complete 4th corner—47 dc on each side. End off.

Rnd 3: From right side, with lp of B on hook, sl st into any corner sp, ch 6, dc in same sp for corner, * ch 2, dc in next dc, ch 2, sk 1 dc, dc in next dc, ** ch 2, sk 2 dc, dc in next dc, repeat from ** 13 times—to within 2 sts of corner—ch 2, sk 1 dc, dc in next dc, ch 2, dc, ch 3, dc all in corner sp, repeat from * around, end with dc in last dc, ch 2, join with sl st in 3rd ch of ch 6 at beg of rnd—18 sps each side plus corners.

Rnd 4: Sl st to center of corner sp, ch 6, turn, dc in same sp for corner, †* ch 2, dc in next dc, repeat from * to next corner, ch 2, dc, ch 3, dc all in corner sp, repeat from † around, end with 1 dc in last dc, ch 2, join with sl st in 3rd ch of ch 6 at beg of rnd. Repeat rnd 4, 6 times.

Rnd 11: Sl st to center of corner sp, ch 8, turn, work same as for rnd 4, working 5 ch instead of 3 in each corner sp. End off.

FINISHING: Block each square to about 16½″ x 16½″. Darn in all ends neatly. Arrange squares as illustrated, having 3 squares in width, 4 in length. With care to match sts and keep seams elastic, sew squares tog. Steam lightly.

Nautical Afghan

The nautical afghan in red, white, and blue is composed of twenty blocks in afghan-stitch crochet: five blocks with sailboats, five with anchors, the designs crocheted in, and ten plain blocks of solid blue.

SIZE: 46″ x 73″.

MATERIALS: Sweater and afghan yarn, 15 2-oz. skeins navy (MC), 2 skeins white (W) and 1 skein red (R). Afghan hook size J.

GAUGE: 9 sts = 2″; 7 rows = 2″.

PLAIN BLOCKS (make 10): With MC, ch 50. Work in afghan st (see page 155) on 50 sts for 50 rows. Sl st in each vertical bar across.

TO CHANGE COLORS: Pick up number of lps of first color shown on chart, drop yarn; with new color, pick up specified number of lps. When the same color appears with no more than 2 sts of another color between (e.g., the MC sections each side of the R rope), the first color may be carried across the back of your work. Join new colors (balls or bobbins) as needed. Work lps off with matching color until there is 1 st left of that color, then change colors, picking up new color from underneath dropped strand to prevent hole in work. New color is drawn through 1 lp of previous color and 1 lp of new color. When a color is no longer needed, break off, leaving end long enough to be woven in on wrong side.

SHIP AND ANCHOR BLOCKS (make 5 of each): With MC, ch 50. Following charts, work in afghan st on 50 sts for 50 rows. Sl st in each vertical bar across.

Edging (work around all blocks): Join MC in first row from corner, ch 2 (counts as 1 dc), dc in next row, * ch 2, sk 2 rows, dc in each of next 2 rows, repeat from * to corner; ch 4, dc in corner st (same st as last dc), dc in next st, ** ch 2, sk 2 sts, dc in each of next 2 sts, repeat from ** to next corner, ch 4, dc in first row, dc in next row, repeat from first * around, end ch 4, sl st in top of first dc. End off.

FINISHING: With MC, holding wrong sides of blocks tog and following placement chart for blocks, sl st blocks tog through back lps (touching lps) of corresponding sts.

Join 3 strands of W in any corner; working backward from left to right, sc in corner ch-4 sp, * ch 1, sc in next ch-2 sp, repeat from * around afghan, working sc, ch 1, sc in each corner. Join with sl st in first sc. End off.

⊠ WHITE

▣ RED

□ BLUE·

BOAT		ANCHOR	
	BOAT		ANCHOR
ANCHOR		BOAT	
	ANCHOR		BOAT
BOAT		ANCHOR	

Embroidered Afghans

Cameo Rose Afghan

White squares in afghan stitch, each one embroidered with a rose and border design, are sewn together for a small coverlet. The 11" squares are easy to handle for those who like to carry their needlework with them. Use Orlon or wool yarn for the crochet, needlepoint and crewel yarn for the cross-stitch embroidery. Photo courtesy of Bucilla Needlecraft.

SIZE: About 45" x 67".

MATERIALS: Knitting worsted, 11 4-oz. skeins main color. For embroidery, Persian-type needlepoint and crewel yarn (10-yard skeins), 24 skeins each of dark blue and medium blue; 8 skeins each of dark green, medium coral and dark coral; 6 skeins each of medium green, light green, light coral and red. Afghan hook size G.

GAUGE: 4 sts = 1"; 4 rows = 1". Each square = 11".

SQUARE (make 24): With main color, ch 44 loosely for lower edge. Work even in afghan st (see Afghan Stitch, page 155) on 44 sts for 44 rows.

Last Row: Sl st under 2nd vertical bar and each vertical bar to last st, insert hook under both vertical strands of last st and work last sl st. End off.

FINISHING: Block each square to 11" x 11". Following charts and working in cross stitch (see page 155), embroider 12 squares following chart A and 12 squares following chart B. Arrange squares as shown on diagram. Sew squares tog from right side, using an overhand st, sewing through back lp of sts only. Keep seams elastic.

Edging: Rnd 1: With main color, from right side, sc around afghan, working 3 sc in each corner. Join with sl st in first sc.

Rnd 2: Sc in each sc, 3 sc in each corner st. Join with sl st in first sc. End off.

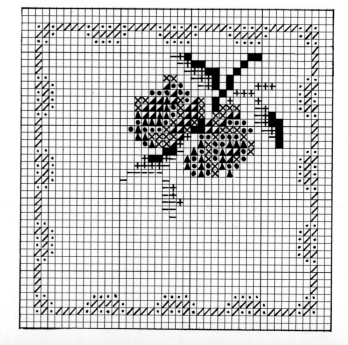

CHART A

CHART B

⊠ DK. CORAL	◙ MED. CORAL	⧅ MED. BLUE	⊞ MED. GREEN	☐ MAIN COLOR
◪ RED	⊡ DK. BLUE	■ DK. GREEN	◭ LT. CORAL	⊟ LT. GREEN

Folk Art Afghan and Pillow

Distelfink birds and flower sprays make charming decorations for an afghan-and-pillow ensemble, so easy in single crochet. The afghan is crocheted in three panels, which are embroidered and then sewn together. Motifs are worked over paper patterns in satin, chain, and outline stitches.

AFGHAN SIZE: 46″ x 66″, plus edgings.

MATERIALS: Orlon yarn of knitting-worsted weight, 11 4-oz. skeins white; 1 2-oz. ball each of marine blue, scarlet, light orange, yellow, Shannon green, and claret (dark red); small amount of black. Crochet hook size H. Large-eyed embroidery needles. One package white crepe paper. Yardstick. Pencil.

GAUGE: 7 sc = 2″; 4 rows = 1″.

Afghan:

CENTER PANEL: With white, ch 75.

Row 1: Sc in 2nd ch from hook and in each ch across—74 sc. Ch 1, turn. Check gauge; piece should be 21″ wide.

Row 2: Sc in each sc across. Ch 1, turn each row. Repeat row 2 until piece is 66″ long. End off.

SIDE PANEL (make 2): With white, ch 43. Work as for center panel on 42 sc. Check gauge; piece should be 12″ wide. Make side panels same length as center panel.

EMBROIDERY: Embroider panels before joining them.

TO ENLARGE DESIGNS: Rule up three 17″ squares of crepe paper into 1″ squares. Enlarge designs for three bird motifs, pages 76–77, to actual size by copying them on crepe paper squares.

Next, rule up a length of crepe paper, 12″ wide x 66″ long, into 1″ squares. Enlarge design for side panel border (one half of design is given, from corner to center), pages 78–79, by copying design on one half of paper's length, then repeat design in reverse for other half of side panel border. Make another piece the same for other side panel.

Finally, rule up a piece of crepe paper, 12″ x 24″, into 1″ squares. Enlarge design for center panel border (p. 78) to actual size by copying on ruled paper. Make another piece the same for other end of center panel.

To Embroider: Baste design in place on afghan. Working through paper and crochet, following color key, embroider birds, flowers, and leaves in satin stitch, stems and birds' legs in outline stitch, heart containing flowers in chain stitch. See pages 154–55 for stitch details.

In placing three bird motifs on center panel, be sure to leave space at top and bottom of center panel for border. Leave borders for top and bottom of center panel until after afghan is put together; then, fit in designs to coincide with side borders.

Finishing: Cut away crepe paper when embroidery is finished.

Join panels by backstitching them together on wrong side, using a narrow seam. Steam-press seams flat. Finish embroidery on top and bottom borders of center panel.

Edging: From right side, join white at beginning of right side edge. Working along side edge, sc evenly across edge to top of afghan, sc in first sc on top edge.

Row 1: Working across top edge, * ch 9, sk 5 sc, sc in next sc, repeat from * across, end sc in last st on top edge. Ch 9, turn.

Row 2: Sl st in center ch of first ch-9 lp, * ch 9, sl st in center ch of next ch-9 lp, repeat from * across, end ch 9, sl st in sc at beg of row 1. Turn.

Row 3: Sl st in each ch to center of first ch-9 lp, * ch 9, sl st in center ch of next ch-9 lp, repeat from * across. Ch 9, turn.

Row 4: Sl st in center ch of first ch-9 lp, * ch 9, sl st in center ch of next ch-9 lp, repeat from * across, end ch 9, sl st in top sl st at beg of row 3. Turn.

Row 5: Sl st in each ch to center of first ch-9 lp, * ch 9, sl st in center ch of next ch-9 lp, repeat from * across. End off.

Work other side edge and bottom edging the same.

Pillows

SIZE: 15″ diameter, plus edging.

MATERIALS: For each pillow, Orlon yarn of knit-

COLOR KEY

S—SCARLET
MB—MARINE BLUE
O—LT. ORANGE
G—SHANNON GREEN
CM—CLARET
B—BLACK
W—WHITE
Y—YELLOW

ting-worsted weight, 2 4-oz. skeins white; 1 oz. each of scarlet, marine blue, light orange, Shannon green, claret; few yards of black. Crochet hook size G. Large-eyed embroidery needles. White crepe paper. Pencil. Round pillow form, 15″ diameter.

GAUGE: 7 sc = 2″; 4 rnds = 1″.

PILLOW (make 2 pieces): Beg at center, with white, ch 3. Sl st in first ch to form ring.

Rnd 1: 6 sc in ring. Do not join rnds; mark end of each rnd.

Rnd 2: 2 sc in each sc around—12 sc.

Rnd 3: * Sc in next sc, 2 sc in next sc, repeat from * around—18 sc.

Rnd 4: * Sc in each of 2 sc, 2 sc in next sc, repeat from * around—24 sc.

Rnd 5: * Sc in each of 3 sc, 2 sc in next sc, repeat from * around—30 sc.

Continue to inc 6 sc each rnd until piece measures 15″

in diameter. End off. Be sure second piece has same number of sts in last rnd as first piece.

TO ENLARGE DESIGNS: Rule up a 15″ square of crepe paper into 1″ squares. Enlarge desired design for pillow to actual size by copying it on crepe paper squares (pages 79–80).

EMBROIDERY: Baste crepe paper design on right side of one crocheted piece, centering design. Working through paper and crochet, following color key, embroider birds, flowers and leaves in satin stitch, stems, birds' legs and heart outline in outline stitch.

Cut away crepe paper when embroidery is finished.

FINISHING: Hold pieces for top and back of pillow wrong sides together. With white, sc pieces together, inserting pillow form before seam is closed. Sl st in first sc, ch 1. Work 1 more rnd of white, 2 rnds of scarlet and 2 rnds of blue, joining each rnd and increasing in every 20th sc to keep work flat. Steam-press edging.

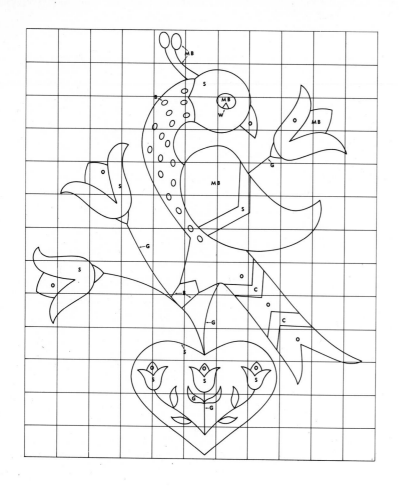

Floral Bouquet Afghan

This floral bouquet afghan has nine solid sections worked in afghan-stitch crochet, joined together with airy mesh insets, and attractively embroidered with sprigs of daisies. Flowers and leaves are embroidered in cross-stitch, stems in outline stitch. Finishing touches: a chain-loop edging, fringes top and bottom. Picture (page 82) courtesy of Bucilla Needlecraft.

SIZE: 50″ x 88″, including fringe.

MATERIALS: Yarn of sweater and afghan type, 18 2-oz. skeins (about 180 yards per skein) blue (A), 1 skein each of white (B), gold (C), and green (D). Afghan hook size H. Crochet hook size F.

GAUGE: 4 sts = 1″; 7 rows = 2″.

AFGHAN: CENTER STRIP: With A and afghan hook, ch 81 for lower border edge. Work in afghan st, using edge st for last st of each row (see page 155) on 81 sts for 48 rows—about 14″ from beg.

Last Row: Sl st under 2nd and each remaining vertical bar to within 1 bar of end, insert hook under both bars and work a final sl st.

Chain-Loop Inset (wrong side): With F hook, ch 1, turn, work sc in first sl st, * ch 5, sk next 3 sts, sc in next st; repeat from * to end—20 ch lps.

Row 2: Ch 5, turn, sc in first lp, * ch 5, sc in next lp, repeat from * to end, ch 2, dc in sc—19 ch lps with 1 half lp at each end.

Row 3: Ch 5, turn, sc in first full lp, * ch 5, sc in next lp; repeat from * to last lp, ch 5, sc in half lp.

Row 4: Repeat row 2, end dc in first ch of ch-5 lp. End off.

Center Afghan-St Panel: Turn, join yarn from right side with H hook, draw up 2 lps in first half lp of ch inset, sk sc, * draw up 4 lps in next ch lp, sk next sc, repeat from * to end, draw up 3 lps in last half ch lp; 81 lps on hook. Work off lps as before. Work afghan st until center panel is 130 rows—about 38″ from beg. Work 1 row sl st. Work inset as before.

Top Afghan-St Border: Work as for center panel for 48 rows. Work a row of sl st. Mark for top.

SIDE STRIPS (make 2): With H hook, ch 49 for lower edge. Working as for center strip, work 48 rows afghan st, 4 rows inset, 130 rows afghan st, 4 rows inset, 48 rows afghan st.

FINISHING: Block strips. Embroider panels in cross st and outline st following charts, page 83. Charts show only completed arrangement of embroidery. Strips have more rows and stitches than shown on chart. For Center Panel, begin embroidery on 5th row from top edge and 41st st in from right edge for center of top flower. On Side Panels, begin embroidery on 12th row from top edge and 15th st in from right edge of right panel for first flower. On Borders, begin embroidery on 18th row from top edge and 14th st from right edge for first leaf.

Inset and Joining Between Strips: From right side, working along side edge of left side strip, with F hook and A, beg at lower edge, work sc in end of first row, * ch 5, sk next 3 rows, sc in end of next row *, repeat between *'s 10 times, ch 5, sc in end of first inset row, ch 5, sc in end of 2nd row of afghan-st panel, 33 lps on afghan-st panel, 2 lps on inset, 12 lps on afghan-st border—61 lps.

Row 2: Repeat row 2 of ch-lp inset. From right side, beg at upper edge of center strip, work 1 row ch lps as for side strip.

Joining Row: Ch 2, turn, work sc in first half lp of left side strip, ch 2, sc in first lp of center strip, * ch 2, sc in next lp of left side strip, ch 2, sc in next lp of center strip, repeat from * to end, ch 2, sc in last half lp of left side strip. Join center and right side strips in same way.

Loop Edging: From right side, join A at upper left corner, work 1 row of ch lps around all 4 sides of afghan.

FRINGE: Wind A around a 10″ cardboard; cut at one end. Fold in half and knot a 6-strand fringe into each lp at upper and lower edges. Steam lightly.

EMBROIDERY CHARTS FOR FLORAL BOUQUET

CENTER PANEL

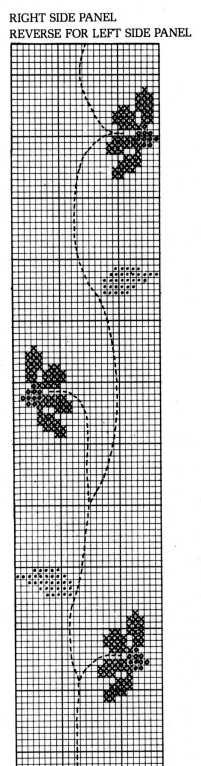

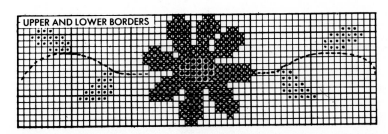

UPPER AND LOWER BORDERS

COLOR-STITCH KEY

- ⊠ B—CROSS-STITCH
- ◉ C—CROSS-STITCH
- ⊡ D—CROSS-STITCH
- – – – D—OUTLINE STITCH
- ∿∿∿ B—OUTLINE STITCH

Florentine Afghan

Reminiscent of Florentine needlepoint, this beautiful afghan is almost completely embroidered in cross-stitch on afghan crochet panels.

SIZE: About 54″ x 72″.

MATERIALS: Orlon yarn of knitting-worsted weight, 13 4-oz. balls of brown (MC). For embroidery, 1 ball each of baby yellow (A), old gold (B), Roman gold (C), pale olive (D), medium olive (E), baby blue (F), Wedgwood blue (G), marine blue (H), rose (I), China rose (J), burgundy (K). Afghan hook size I. Crochet hook size H. Tapestry needles.

GAUGE: 4 sts = 1″; 3 rows = 1″.

Note: Afghan can be made in one piece or in 3 separate panels.

ONE-PIECE AFGHAN: With MC, ch 223. Work in afghan stitch on 223 sts, following directions, page 155, until 221 rows have been completed. Work sl st in each vertical bar across. End off.

AFGHAN IN PANELS: With MC, ch 71. Work in afghan stitch on 71 sts, following directions, page 155, until 221 rows have been completed. Work sl st in each vertical bar across. End off. Make one more panel the same.

For center panel, with MC, ch 81. Work in afghan stitch on 81 sts until 221 rows have been completed. Work sl st in each vertical bar across. End off.

FINISHING: If afghan is made in panels, sew panels tog with MC, having wider panel in center. With MC, work 1 row sc along each long edge of afghan. Following chart, embroider afghan in cross-stitch: work from A to B twice, then from A to C once. When top of chart is reached, repeat from bottom of chart twice, then repeat from bottom of chart until top of afghan is reached. Steam.

FRINGE: Cut strands of all colors 10″. Using 2 strands of MC and 1 strand each of 3 colors, knot fringe in every other st across top and bottom of afghan, alternating the 4 color groups. Trim ends.

□ = MC
▧ = A
◉ = B
⊠ = C
⊡ = D
◹ = E
▽ = F
⊞ = G
⊟ = H
◣ = I
▣ = J
◿ = K

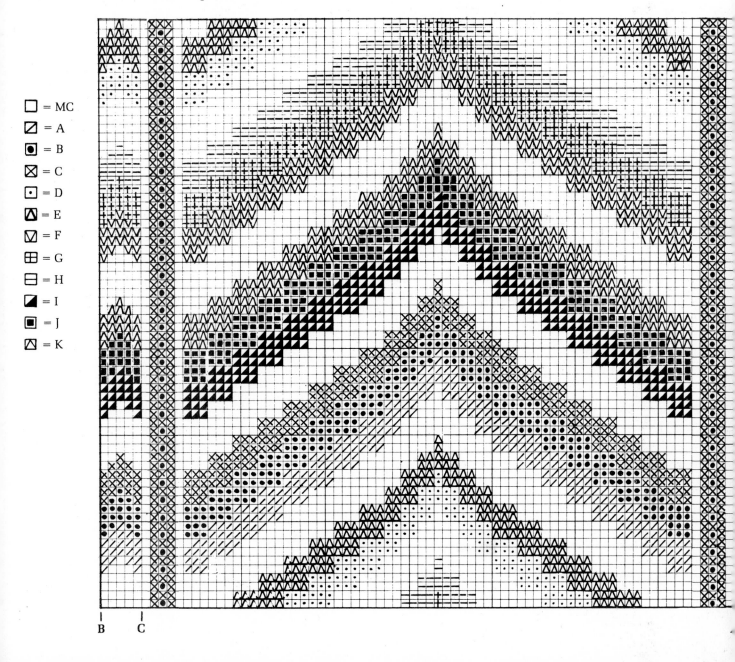

B   C

Nostalgia Afghan

Crocheted and cross-stitched afghan is an old design. Panels of red, bottle green, white, and black are worked in afghan stitch and embroidered with roses, leaves, and scrolls.

SIZE: 60″ x 45″, plus fringe.

MATERIALS: Knitting worsted, 4 4-oz. balls each of geranium red and bottle green, 3 balls of black and 2 balls of oyster white. Afghan hook size G or 5. For embroidery: Knitting worsted, 1 2-oz. ball each of scarlet, burgundy, medium olive, light olive, myrtle green, green mist, tapestry green, honey, cinnamon, walnut and luggage. Tapestry needle.

GAUGE: 5 sts = 1″; 4 rows = 1″.

AFGHAN STITCH: Make a chain with same number of ch sts as desired number of afghan sts.

Row 1: Sk first ch from hook, pull up a lp in next ch and in each remaining ch, keeping all lps on hook.

To Work Lps Off: Yo hook, pull through first lp, * yo hook, pull through next 2 lps, repeat from * across. Lp that remains on hook always counts as first st of next row.

Row 2: Sk first vertical bar of row below, pull up a lp under next vertical bar and under each vertical bar across. Work lps off as before. Repeat row 2 for afghan stitch.

AFGHAN: Green Panel (make 2): With bottle green, ch 48. Work in afghan st on 48 sts for 171 rows. Piece should be about 9½″ wide. Ch 1, sk first vertical bar of last row, sc under next vertical bar and under each vertical bar across top of panel, 3 sc in corner, sc in end st of each row to bottom of panel, 3 sc in corner, sc in each ch of starting ch, 3 sc in corner, sc in end st of each row to top of panel. End off.

Red Panel (make 2): With geranium red, ch 38. Work in afghan st on 38 sts for 171 rows. Piece should be about 7½″ wide. Work 1 row of sc around panel as for green panel.

White Panel (make 2): With oyster white, ch 22. Work in afghan st on 22 sts for 171 rows. Piece should be about 4½″ wide. Work 1 row of sc around panel as for green panel.

Black Panel (make 1): With black, ch 60. Work in afghan st on 60 sts for 171 rows. Piece should be about 12″ wide. Work 1 row of sc around panel as for green panel.

EMBROIDERY: Block panels to same length before embroidering. Embroider designs in cross-stitch before assembling panels. Use knitting worsted single for embroidery. Following charts on pages 88–89, work designs from bottom to top of panels. Each square on chart represents 1 cross-stitch worked over 1 afghan st; see detail (page 155). For black, oyster white, geranium red and bottle green embroidery, use background yarns.

Green Panels: Embroider both panels the same. First count off 11 sts from right-hand edge of panel, place a pin between 11th and 12th sts. Pin marks right-hand edge of Chart 1. First cross-stitch on bottom row of Chart 1 is worked over 6th st from pin marker. Following Chart 1 and starting in 2nd row of crochet, work from row 1 to row 142, then repeat rows 4 to 30.

Red Panels: Embroider one red panel with oak leaf design. First count off 7 sts from right-hand edge of panel, place pin between 7th and 8th sts. Pin marks right-hand edge of Chart 2. First cross-stitch on bottom row of chart is worked over 15th st from pin marker. Following Chart 2 and starting in 2nd row of crochet, work from row 1 to row 83, then repeat from row 8 to top of chart.

Embroider 2nd red panel with maple leaf design. First count off 6 sts from right-hand edge of panel, place a pin between 6th and 7th sts. Pin marks right-hand edge of Chart 3. First cross-stitch on bottom row of chart is worked over 10th st from pin marker. Following Chart 3 and starting in 2nd row of crochet, work from row 1 to row 98, then repeat from row 6 to row 74 and complete design that shows below dark line at left of chart.

White Panels: Embroider both panels the same. First count off 6 sts from right-hand edge of panel, place a pin between 6th and 7th sts. Pin marks right-hand edge of Chart 4. First cross-stitch on bottom row of chart is worked over the 2nd st from pin marker. Following Chart 4 and starting in 2nd row of crochet, repeat the 20 rows of chart 8 times, then repeat first 9 rows.

Black Panel: Count off 10 sts from right-hand edge of panel, place a pin between 10th and 11th sts. Pin marks right-hand edge of Chart 5. First cross-stitch on bottom row of chart is worked over 2nd st from pin marker. Following Chart 5 and starting in 2nd row of crochet, work from row 1 to row 86, then repeat from row 3 to row 79 and complete rose design that shows below dark line at left of chart.

FINISHING: Green panels are placed at sides of afghan, then red panels, then white panels, with black panel at center. To join panels, place two panels tog, right

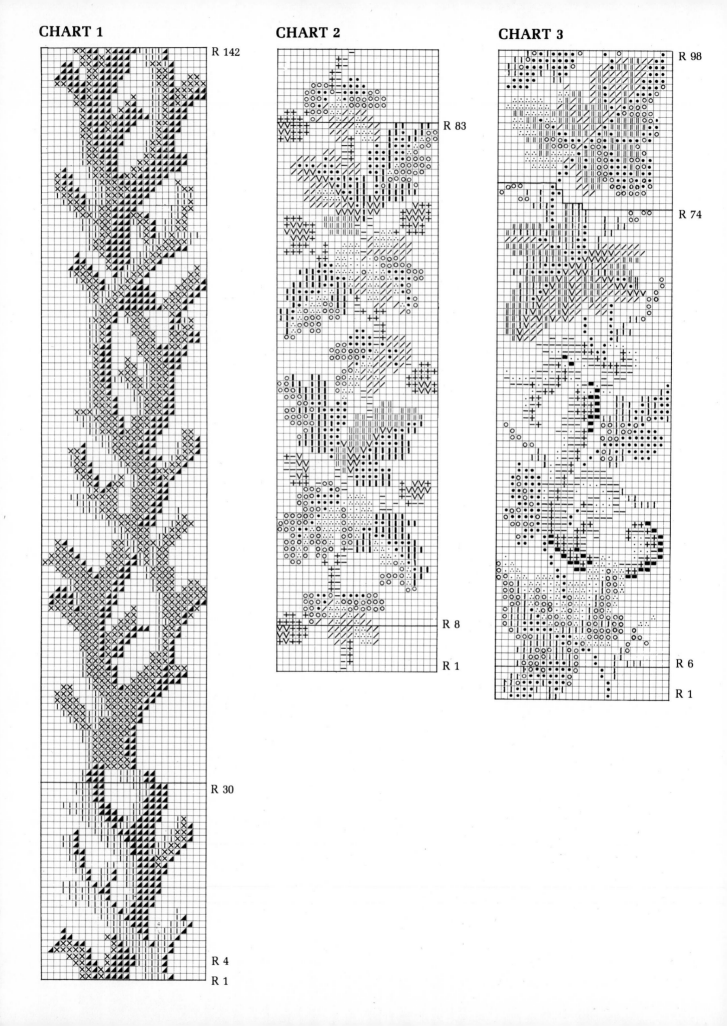

CHART 1

R 142

R 30

R 4
R 1

CHART 2

R 83

R 8

R 1

CHART 3

R 98

R 74

R 6

R 1

sides out. Join color of one panel in first sc at bottom of panel facing you. Working up side, ch 3 for first dc, work 1 dc in each of first 5 sc of one panel. Beg in 6th sc of other panel, work 1 dc in each of 5 sc. * Sk 5 sc of first panel, work 1 dc in each of next 5 sc, sk 5 sc of other panel, work 1 dc in each of next 5 sc, repeat from * to top. End off. Turn work around. With color of other panel, starting at end just finished, join yarn in first sc, ch 3 for first dc; remove hook from lp, insert it through top of last dc on opposite side and pull lp through. * Dc in next sc, remove hook, insert hook in top of next dc on opposite side and pull lp through. Repeat from * across, working in each free sc. End off.

FRINGE: Cut yarn of all four background colors into 16″ lengths. Holding 5 strands of green tog, fold strands in half. With hook, pull folded end through sc at bottom edge of green panel, forming a loop; pull ends through loop; tighten knot. Knot a fringe in every 4th sc across panel. With matching yarn, knot fringe in same way across bottom and top of afghan, spacing fringes evenly. On sides, knot fringe in same way, alternating colors: green, red, black, white.

To Tie: * Take 5 strands of one fringe and 5 strands of adjacent fringe. Knot tog 1″ below first knot; repeat from * around. Separate strands below second knot. Knot tog 5 strands of one fringe and 5 strands of adjacent fringe 1″ below second knot. (On sides, keep 5 strands of one color tog.) Trim fringe evenly all around afghan.

■ BLACK
☐ OYSTER WHITE
☒ BOTTLE GREEN
▥ MEDIUM OLIVE
◉ MYRTLE GREEN
◫ LIGHT OLIVE
⊡ GREEN MIST
⊞ TAPESTRY GREEN
☑ HONEY (YELLOW)
◫ SCARLET
☒ GERANIUM RED
◪ BURGUNDY
⊟ CINNAMON
⊞ WALNUT
◳ LUGGAGE

CHART 4

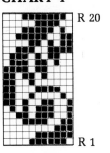

R 20

R 1

CHART 5

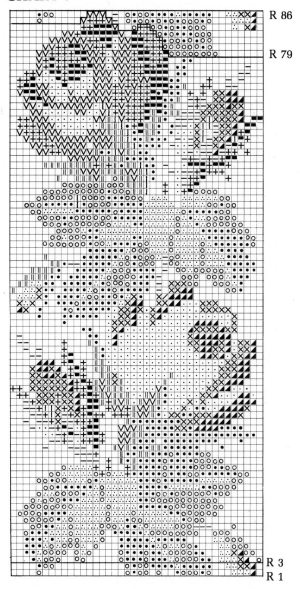

R 86

R 79

R 3
R 1

Treasure Chest Afghan

This Victorian heirloom combines five afghan-stitch panels and four knitted cable-stitch stripes. Rich embroidery on the crocheted panels is in half cross-stitch, resembling needlepoint.

SIZE: 60″ wide x 57″ long, plus fringe.

MATERIALS: Sport yarn, 4-ply 10 2-oz. skeins gold, 10 skeins scarlet, 5 skeins ivy green, 2 skeins orange rust, 1 skein yellow. Afghan hook size F or 3. Crochet hook size F or 3. Set of double-pointed needles No. 1. For embroidery: tapestry wool, crewel wool, knitting worsted, or sport yarn used double, in the following colors: peach, pale red, medium rose red, dark rose red, burgundy, pale yellow, light gold, medium gold, taupe, black, bronze, light olive, medium olive, dark olive, light blue green, medium blue green, dark blue green, very dark blue green, grass green, slate blue, tan. Tapestry needles.

GAUGE: 6 sts = 1″; 6 rows = 1″.

AFGHAN: First Panel (make 2): With gold and afghan hook, ch 60.

Row 1: Pull up a lp in 2nd ch from hook and in each ch across—60 lps on hook. Work lps off as follows: yo hook, pull through first lp, * yo hook, pull through next 2 lps, repeat from * across—60 sts; 1 lp remains on hook and counts as first st of next row.

Row 2: Sk first vertical bar, pull up a lp in each vertical bar across—60 lps on hook. Work lps off: yo hook, pull through first lp, * yo hook, pull through next 2 lps, repeat from * across—60 sts; 1 lp remains on hook. Check gauge; piece should measure 10″ wide. Repeat row 2 until there are 342 rows. Piece should be about 57″ long. End off.

Second Panel (make 2): With scarlet, work as for first panel.

Center Panel: With ivy green, work as for first panel.

EMBROIDERY: Embroider panels following individual directions and charts on page 92 before joining them. See stitch details on page 155. Work all embroidery in half cross-stitch (except for flower centers on gold panels, worked in cross-stitch), working each stitch diagonally over one vertical bar of afghan stitch.

Gold Panels: In illustration, gold panels were embroidered with ombre yarn in shaded reds. Use shaded reds if available; if not, use peach, pale red, medium rose red, dark rose red and burgundy, using colors in shaded fashion as shown, page 92. One gold panel has four cross-stitches at center of each flower as shown on chart; other gold panel has a single cross-stitch at center of each flower. Use either or both styles, as

desired. Beginning at lower edge of panel on 9th row from bottom, embroider design on center 13 sts of panel (there will be 24 plain sts on one side, 23 plain sts on other side). Start at row 1 of Chart 1, work to row 26, then repeat from row 3 to row 26 12 times, then work last 11 rows of flower, omitting 2 sts at right top corner of flower.

Scarlet Panels: Mark lower edge of design on panel with pins or basting thread between 20th and 21st row of panel. Mark right-hand edge of design between 5th and 6th sts. Markings indicate placement of first flower. Embroider one panel following Chart 2 and one panel following Chart 3. Leave 13 rows free between flowers.

Green Panel: Mark right-hand edge of design on panel with pins or basting thread between 6th and 7th sts. Marking indicates right-hand edge of Chart 4. Beginning in 3rd row from bottom of panel, embroider panel following Chart 4 from row 1 to row 160, then repeat from row 7 to row 160. Repeat from row 7 to top of panel, leaving one or two rows free at top.

CABLE STRIPS (make 4): With orange rust and double-pointed needles No. 1, cast on 14 sts. K 1 row.

Row 1 (right side): K 5, turn; (p 4, turn; k 4, turn) twice, p 4, turn; k 4, sl next 4 sts to another dp needle, hold in back of work, k last 5 sts.

Row 2: P 9, p 4 from dp needle, p last st.

Row 3: K across—14 sts.

Row 4: P 5, turn; (k 4, turn; p 4, turn) twice, k 4, turn; p 4, sl next 4 sts to dp needle, hold in front of work, p last 5 sts.

Row 5: K 9, k 4 sts from dp needle, k last st.

Row 6: P across—14 sts. Repeat rows 1-6 until strip measures same as crocheted panels. Bind off.

FINISHING: Steam-press pieces.

Joining Edge: With yellow and crochet hook, from right side, work 1 row of sc along side edges of scarlet and green panels, working 1 sc in each end st—342 sc each edge. Repeat on inside edge only of each gold panel. With ivy green, work 1 row of sc along side edges of all cable strips, working 342 sc on each edge—about 6 sc to 1″. Join crocheted panels to knitted strips as follows: Hold knitted strip behind crocheted panel, wrong sides tog, edges even. With ivy green, make lp on hook. Sc edges tog for 4 sts; begin 5th sc, drop green, pull lp of yellow through 2 lps on hook. * Working over green strand, work 5 sc in yellow, changing to green on 5th st; working over yellow strand, work 5 sc in green, changing to yellow on 5th st; repeat from *, joining edges.

Side Edging: From right side, work along outer edge of each gold panel as follows: With gold, make lp on hook, sc in end st of first row, * ch 3, sk 3 rows, sc in end st of next row, repeat from * across. With scarlet, make lp on hook; join with sl st in first ch-3 lp; ch 3, dc in first ch-3 lp, ch 2, sc in top of dc for picot, (dc in same ch-3 lp, ch 2, sc in top of last dc made, for picot) 3 times, sk next ch-3 lp, sc over sc between lps into end st of panel, * sk next ch-3 lp; in next ch-3 lp, work shell of 8 dc with 8 picots, sk next ch-3 lp, sc over sc between lps into end st of panel, repeat from * across, end with half shell of 4 dc

CHART 1

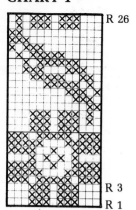

R 26

R 3
R 1

⊠ SHADED REDS

CHART 2

CHART 3

CHART 4

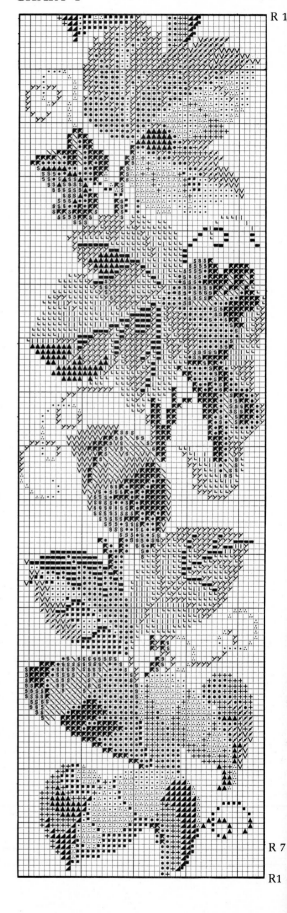

R 1

R 7

R1

■ BLACK
◹ PALE RED
Ⓢ MED. ROSE RED
◪ DK. ROSE RED
◉ BURGUNDY
⊡ PALE YELLOW
⊞ LT. GOLD
▽ MED. GOLD
Ⓦ TAUPE
▲ BRONZE
Ⓛ LT. OLIVE
⊠ MED. OLIVE
⊟ DK. OLIVE
⊡ LT. BLUE GREEN
◩ MED. BLUE GREEN
⊞ DK. BLUE GREEN
◪ VERY DK. BLUE GREEN
◎ GRASS GREEN
⊠ SLATE BLUE
◪ TAN

with 4 picots in last ch-3 lp, ch 3, sl st in last lp. End off.

Top and Bottom Edging: From right side, work along top edge of afghan as follows: With gold, make lp on hook, sc in first st of gold panel, * ch 3, sk 2 sts, sc in next st, repeat from * across gold panel; end off. Join orange rust in same st as last gold st, work 5 ch-3 lps across joining edges and knitted strip, end in first st of scarlet panel. Join scarlet in same st as last orange rust st, work ch-3 lps across scarlet panel as for gold panel. Continue across top, working ch-3 lps to match panels. Repeat on bottom edge.

FRINGE: Cut strands 20″ long to match panels (wind yarn around 10″ cardboard, cut through strands at one edge).

First Row of Knots: Hold 5 strands tog, fold strands in half, pull folded end through matching ch-3 lp, pull 10 ends through lp; tighten knot. Knot a fringe in each ch-3 lp across top and bottom edges.

Second Row of Knots: Separate first fringe into 2 groups of 5 strands. Repeat with second fringe. With 5 strands of first fringe and 5 strands of second fringe tog, make a knot ¾″ below first row of knots. With remaining 5 strands of second fringe and 5 strands of third fringe tog, make a knot ¾″ below first row of knots. Repeat across, knotting pairs of strand groups.

Third Row of Knots: Separate second fringe into 2 groups of 5 strands. With 5 strands of first fringe and 5 strands of second fringe tog, make a knot ¾″ below second row of knots. Continue across, knotting pairs of strand groups.

Victorian Carriage Robe

This nineteenth-century carriage robe was embroidered in a gloriously Victorian style by a New Englander, perhaps for her parson. The basic robe is worked in afghan crochet—a separate section for the center, eight sections for the border. Each section is embroidered in cross-stitch, then joined for the 58" x 71" afghan. If you prefer, substitute another dog's head for the religious symbol. Put a new date in the corner.

SIZE: 58" x 71", plus fringe.

MATERIALS: Knitting worsted, 16 4-oz. skeins black for background; 1 skein each of the following colors for embroidery (or use tapestry wool, crewel wool, or left-over yarns):

Four reds: pale red, light red, medium red, cardinal.

Three purples: lavender, light purple, dark purple.

Three old-rose tones: light old rose, medium old rose, dark old rose.

Four greens: pale almond green, light almond green, medium almond green, dark almond green.

Four beige tones (white rose): oyster white, natural heather, celery, camel.

Four yellow-browns: tobacco gold, copper, wood brown, dark wood brown.

Two rusts: dark apricot, rust.

Yellow.

Five tans (horse and dogs): parchment, pale russet brown, light russet brown, medium russet brown, dark russet brown.

14" aluminum afghan hook size 9 or J. Tapestry needles No. 17. Large-eyed rug needle.

GAUGE: 7 sts = 2"; 7 rows = 2".

CENTER SECTION: Ch 155. Work in afghan st (see page 155) on 155 sts for 112 rows. Piece should measure 44¼" wide, 32" long.

Next Row: Sl st loosely under 2nd vertical bar and in each vertical bar across. End off.

Mark between 17th and 18th sts from right edge for right edge of cross-stitch design. Mark between 11th and 12th rows from bottom for bottom edge of design. Following chart, page 96, embroider horse in cross-stitch.

SIDE ROSE BORDERS (make 2): Ch 112. Work in afghan st on 112 sts for 46 rows. Piece should measure 32" wide, 13" deep.

Next Row: Sl st loosely under 2nd vertical bar and in each bar across. End off.

Mark between 3rd and 4th sts from right edge for right edge of design. Mark between 3rd and 4th rows for bottom of design. Following Chart 1, page 97, embroider rose border.

TOP AND BOTTOM ROSE BORDERS (make 2): Ch 155. Work in afghan st on 155 sts for 46 rows. Piece should measure 44¼" wide, 13" deep.

Next Row: Sl st loosely under 2nd vertical bar and in each bar across. End off.

Mark between 4th and 5th sts from right edge for right edge of design. Mark between 3rd and 4th rows for bottom of design. Following Chart 2, embroider rose border from A to B, then repeat end rose only from C to D.

CORNERS (make 4): Ch 46. Work in afghan st on 46 sts for 46 rows. Piece should be 13" square.

Next Row: Sl st loosely under 2nd vertical bar and in each bar across. End off.

Dog Heads: Mark between 8th and 9th sts from right edge for right edge of design. Starting in 4th row, following chart, page 98, embroider head in cross-stitch. For second corner (top right), follow first corner, reversing design.

Monogram of Jesus: Mark between 6th and 7th sts from right edge for right edge of design. Starting in first row, following chart, embroider monogram in cross-stitch.

Date: Using illustration of afghan as guide, plan date to fit space. Use graph paper, if necessary, to work out most pleasing arrangement of letters and numbers.

FINISHING: Weave in yarn ends on wrong side. Pin out pieces to correct measurements; steam-press. When pieces are dry, sew them together with black yarn. Cover joinings with cross-stitch in palest tone of horse. With same tone, work 1 row of sc around edge, making sc in each st or row, 3 sc in each corner. Join in first sc; end off.

FRINGE: Row 1: Use 4 strands of black yarn, cut 24" long, in large-eyed rug needle. Hold afghan right side up with edge of afghan toward you. Bring needle up from wrong side through a st on edge. Pull yarn through leaving 2" end in back. Hold this 2" end in left hand.

Put needle from right to left under end in left hand,

bring it up forming loop at right. Insert needle from top to bottom through loop; pull tight, forming knot on edge. Drop 2″ end. * Skip 3 sc to left on edge, bring needle up from wrong side through next st on edge. Pull yarn through forming scallop of yarn on edge. Insert needle from front to back through scallop. Pull yarn through forming loop. Insert needle from top to bottom through loop (see Fringe Detail, page 99); pull tight, forming knot on edge. Repeat from * around edge. Weave in ends on wrong side.

Row 2: Thread 4 strands of black yarn in large-eyed needle. Tie yarn in center of any scallop, leaving 3″ end. Working from right to left as before, * bring yarn up through next scallop and down through scallop just formed, forming a loop. Insert needle from top to bottom through loop; pull tight, forming knot. Repeat from * around, alternating one deep scallop with one scallop straight across. Finish off strands by tying knot and leaving 3″ of yarn hanging. Start new strands with a knot on next scallop, leaving 3″ of yarn hanging. Tie these ends together in a deep scallop and cut ends close.

Finish each deep scallop with a tassel of yarn tied to

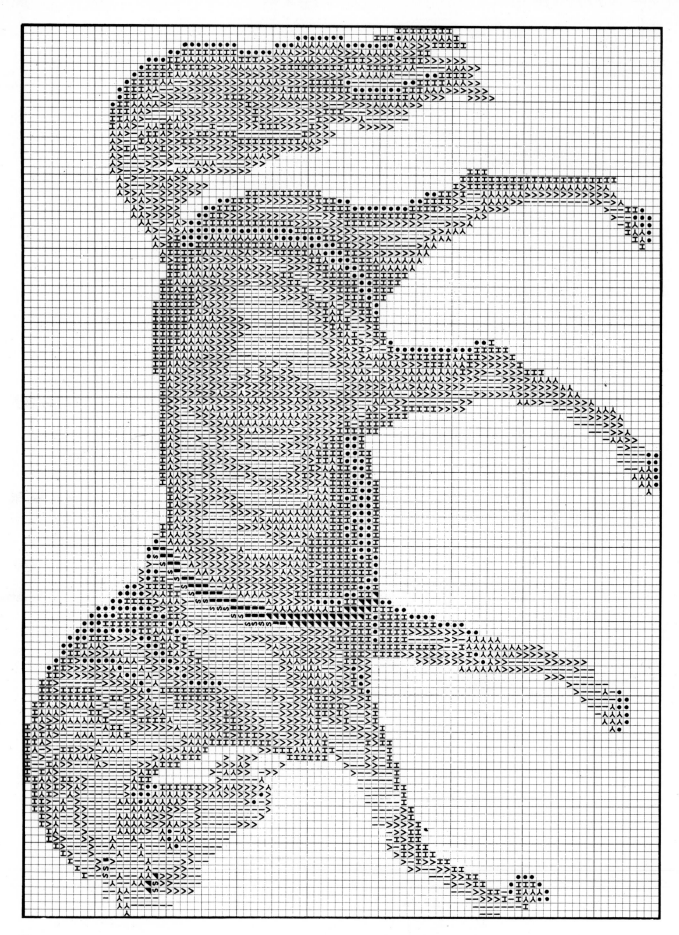

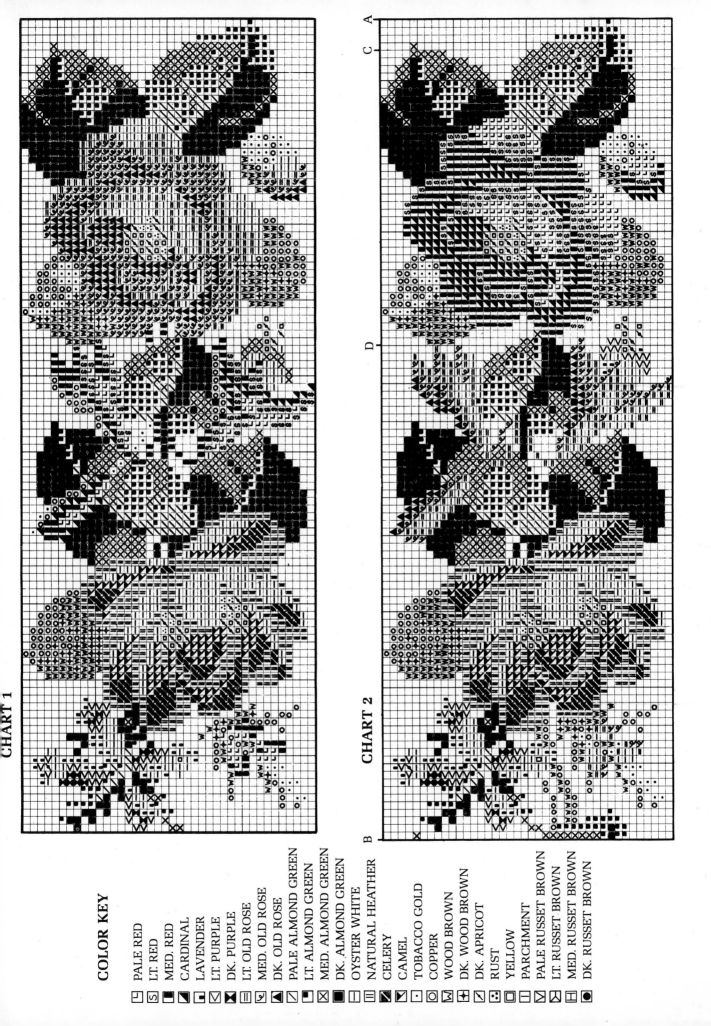

CHART 1

CHART 2

COLOR KEY

⊔	PALE RED
⑤	LT. RED
■	MED. RED
◣	CARDINAL
▽	LAVENDER
✕	LT. PURPLE
⊟	DK. PURPLE
◪	LT. OLD ROSE
◀	MED. OLD ROSE
◥	DK. OLD ROSE
■	PALE ALMOND GREEN
✕	LT. ALMOND GREEN
■	MED. ALMOND GREEN
‖	DK. ALMOND GREEN
⫽	OYSTER WHITE
◸	NATURAL HEATHER
·	CELERY
○	CAMEL
◎	TOBACCO GOLD
✛	COPPER
◿	WOOD BROWN
◌	DK. WOOD BROWN
▯	DK. APRICOT
▯	RUST
▽	YELLOW
◩	PARCHMENT
◿	PALE RUSSET BROWN
⊞	LT. RUSSET BROWN
⊟	MED. RUSSET BROWN
●	DK. RUSSET BROWN

center of scallop. To make tassel, wind several strands of yarn of different colors around a 3″ piece of cardboard 4 or 5 times. Slide a strand of yarn under one edge and knot it as tightly as possible to hold strands together. Cut through yarn on opposite edge. Wrap and tie a strand of yarn around tassel 1″ from top. Tie tassel to scallop by inserting threaded needle up through tassel, over scallop, then back through tassel. Knot yarn close to wound part of tassel, clip even with bottom of tassel.

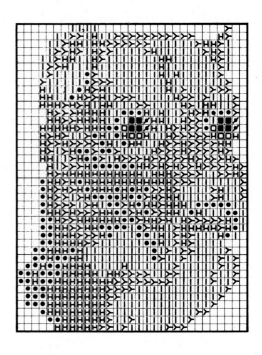

COLOR KEY

- ⊓ PARCHMENT
- � V PALE RUSSET BROWN
- ⋈ LT. RUSSET BROWN
- ⊞ MED. RUSSET BROWN
- ⊙ DK. RUSSET BROWN
- ■ DK. ALMOND GREEN
- ⧄ DK. APRICOT
- ⊡ YELLOW

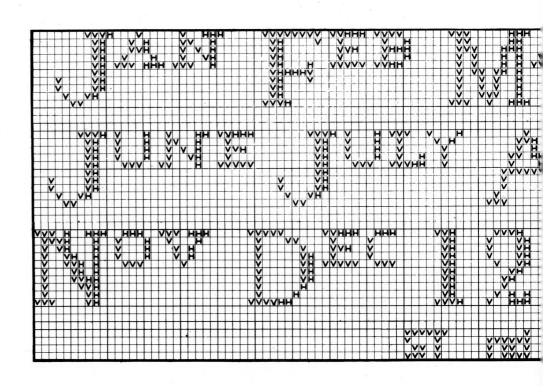

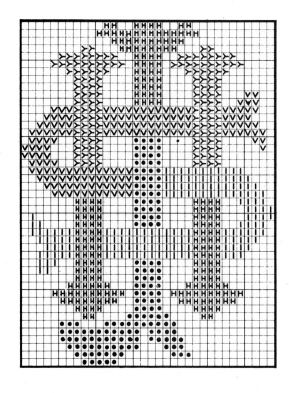

FRINGE DETAIL

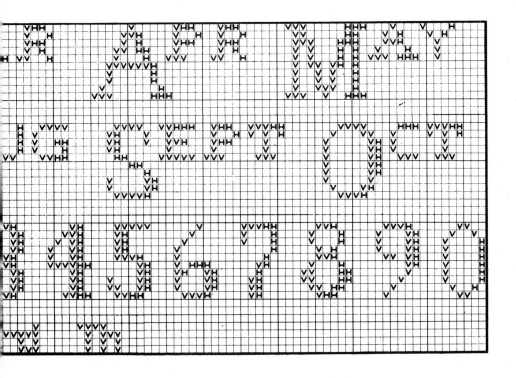

Seashells Afghan

The watery world of seaweed and shells inspired this pale green-blue afghan. The three panels used as background for the cross-stitch embroidery are in afghan-stitch crochet. Openwork panels, made separately and sewn between the shell-embroidered sections, add a contrasting lacy and three-dimensional texture.

SIZE: 46″ x 62″.

MATERIALS: Yarn of sweater and afghan type (about 180 yards per skein), 13 2-oz. skeins aqua (A), 1 skein each of winter white (B), brown (C), green (D), melon (E). Afghan hook size J. Crochet hook size H.

GAUGE: 4 sts = 1″; 3 rows = 1″.

AFGHAN-ST PANEL (make 3): With A and afghan hook, ch 40. Work even in afghan st (see page 155) on 40 sts for 181 rows, about 60″ from beg. Mark first row of panel for lower edge.

Last Row: Work sl st in each vertical bar across. End off. Block each panel to 10″ x 62″.

OPENWORK PANEL (make 2): With A and size H hook, ch 34 loosely.

Row 1 (right side): Sc in 2nd ch from hook, * ch 1, sk next ch, sc in next ch, repeat from * across—33 sts.

Row 2: Ch 4, turn, sk first ch-1 sp, dc in front lp of next sc, * ch 1, sk next ch-1 sp, dc in front lp of next sc, repeat from * across—33 sts; 16 sps.

Row 3: Ch 1, turn, sc in front lp of first dc, * ch 1, sk ch-1 sp, sc in front lp of next dc, repeat from * across, end ch 1, sk 1 ch of turning ch 4, sc in next ch. Repeat rows 2 and 3 until there are 121 rows, about 60″ from beg, end with row 3. End off. Mark first row for lower edge. Block each panel to 8″ x 62″.

EMBROIDERY: See page 155 for cross-stitch on afghan st, outline st and French knot. Beg on 16th row from lower edge, embroider one panel following chart for center panel. Beg on 13th row from lower edge, embroider two panels following chart for side panels, page 102.

FINISHING: Arrange panels as shown in photograph. With A, sew panels tog from right side, using over-hand st and sewing 2 rows of openwork panel to 3 rows of afghan-st panel, keeping seam as elastic as crochet fabric.

With A and size H hook, from right side, work 1 row sc around entire afghan, keeping work flat and working 3 sc in each corner; join with sl st in first sc. End off.

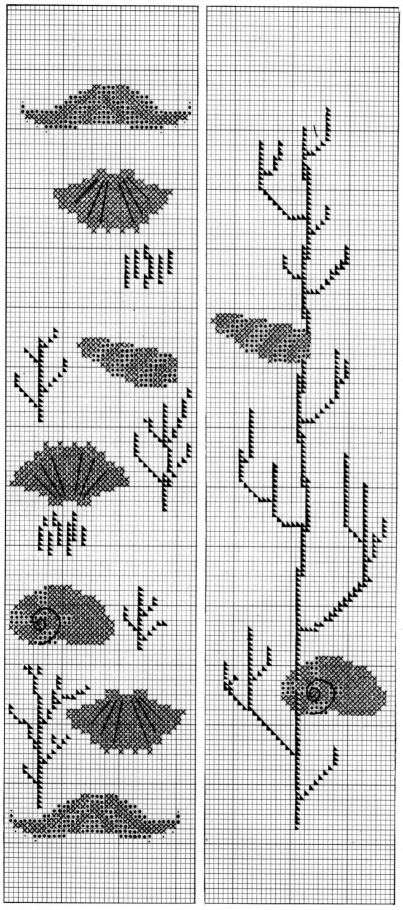

CHART 1 **CHART 2**

□ = A
⊠ = B
⊡ = C
◨ = D
⊡ = E

Birds in Flight Afghan

Bold birds in flight alternate with wavy stripes for a dramatic design. Five wide and narrow panels are worked in afghan crochet; then the panels are embroidered in cross-stitch, edged, and joined for the 72"-long afghan.

SIZE: 52" x 72".

MATERIALS: Knitting worsted, 10 4-oz. skeins turquoise, main color (MC); 2 skeins white (A); 1 skein each of kelly green (B), light navy (C) and black (D). Afghan hook size G or No. 6. Tapestry needle.

GAUGE: 9 sts = 2"; 3 rows = 1".

AFGHAN: WIDE STRIP (make 2): With MC, ch 56.
Row 1: Keeping all lps on hook, sk first ch from hook (lp on hook is first st), pull up a lp in each ch across—56 lps.

To Work Lps Off: Yo hook, pull through first lp, * yo hook, pull through next 2 lps, repeat from * until 1 lp remains. Lp that remains on hook always counts as first st of next row.

Row 2: Keeping all lps on hook, sk first vertical bar, pull up a lp in next vertical bar and under each vertical bar across. Work lps off as before. Repeat row 2 until 209 rows from start. Sl st in each vertical bar across. End off. Check gauge; piece should measure 12½″ wide, 70″ long.

NARROW STRIP (make 3): With MC, ch 24. Work same as for wide strip. Check gauge; piece should measure 5½″ wide.

EMBROIDERY: Note: Each square on charts is one stitch; each row on charts is one row of afghan st (lps pulled up on hook and worked off).

Wide Strips: Beg on row 14, embroider Chart 1 in cross-st; beg on row 85, embroider Chart 2; beg on row 156, embroider Chart 1.

Narrow Strips: Beg on row 2, work and repeat the 22 rows of Chart 3, end on row 208.

Edging: Row 1: With C, make lp on hook. From right side, working on side edge of wide strip, * sc in each of 3 rows, long dc under bar of st 2 rows below edge, repeat from * across. End.

Row 2: With B, make lp on hook. From right side, sc in back lp of each of 2 sc, * long dc, inserting hook at base of next sc, sc in back lp of next 3 sts, repeat from * across. End off.

Row 3: With A, make lp on hook. From right side, sc in back lp of first sc, work from first * to 2nd * of row 2. End off.

Row 4: With D, make lp on hook. From right side, sc in each of 4 sc, work from first * to 2nd * of row 2. End off.

Work same edging on each side edge of wide strips, each side edge of one narrow strip (center strip), one side edge of remaining 2 narrow strips.

Join Strips: With D, working through back lps, weave a wide strip to edges of center narrow strip, having birds face opposite direction. Weave a narrow strip to each wide strip.

Work border same as edging around afghan, increasing at corners.

CHART 1

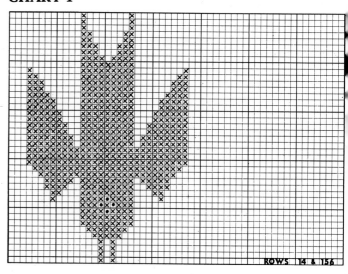

ROWS 14 & 156

CHART 2

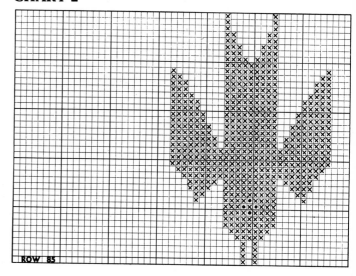

ROW 85

COLOR KEY

☐ MC
☒ A
☑ B
◉ C
⬤ D

CHART 3

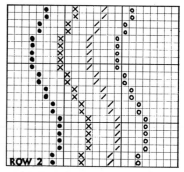

ROW 2

Cowboy Afghan

A bold and cheerful afghan for a child's room features a rodeo cowboy embroidered in cross-stitch on an afghan-stitch background. If you wish, substitute a favorite embroidery motif in the colors of your choice. The striped border, in double crochet, picks up the embroidery colors.

SIZE: About 44″ x 50″.

MATERIALS: Knitting worsted, 12 oz. yellow, main color (MC); 6 oz. each blue (A), brown (B), black (C), white (D) and red (E). Afghan hook size J. Crochet hook size G. Tapestry needle.

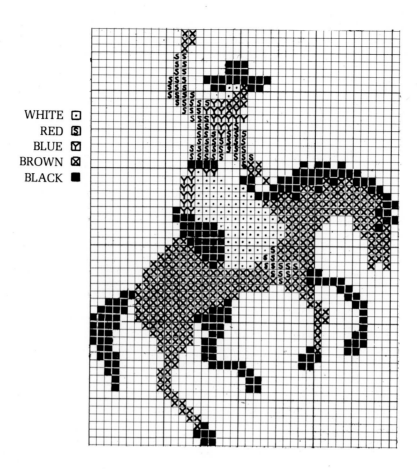

WHITE ☐
RED Ⓢ
BLUE ⓨ
BROWN ⊠
BLACK ■

GAUGE: 7 sts = 2″; 3 rows = 1″ (afghan st). 3 dc = 1″; 3 dc rows = 2″.

AFGHAN: CENTER SECTION (20″ x 26″): With MC and afghan hook, ch 70.

Row 1: Pull up a lp in 2nd ch from hook and in each ch across, keeping all lps on hook.

To Work Off Lps: Yo hook, pull through first lp, * yo hook, pull through next 2 lps, repeat from * across until 1 lp remains. Lp that remains on hook always counts as first st of next row.

Row 2: Keeping all lps on hook, pull up a lp under 2nd vertical bar and under each vertical bar across—70 lps. Work off lps as before. Repeat row 2 until there are 78 rows.

Next Row: Sl st loosely under 2nd vertical bar and in each bar across.

EMBROIDERY: With pins, mark off area of center section to be embroidered: place pins between 12th and 13th rows from bottom and top of piece, between 14th and 15th sts from right edge and between 15th and 16th sts from left edge. Following chart, work cross-stitch cowboy on marked area, 41 sts wide and 54 rows long. Each square on chart represents 1 afghan st. Work cross-stitch over vertical bar of st; see page 155.

BORDER: From right side, work around entire center section as follows:

Rnd 1: With A and crochet hook, make lp on hook; beg in a corner st, make 5 dc in each corner, 70 dc across top and bottom edges, 78 dc at each side edge. Join rnd with sl st in first dc. End off A.

Beg and ending each rnd as for rnd 1, and working dc in each dc and 5 dc in each corner st around, work border in following striped pattern (rnd 2 is MC): 1 dc rnd each of A, MC, B, C, D and E. Work border for 15 rnds, then continue for 3 rnds more, making 7 dc in each corner dc. End off.

Knitted Afghans

Pinwheel Afghan

Triangles of four bright colors, joined in pinwheel fashion to black triangles, create an afghan both easy to knit and extra warm, in garter stitch. Twelve pinwheel squares form the afghan.

SIZE: About 51″ x 68″.

MATERIALS: Knitting worsted, 7 4-oz. skeins black, 2 skeins each of yellow, red, blue, and green. Knitting needles No. 8. Steel crochet hook No. 00.

GAUGE: 9 sts = 2″.

TRIANGLE: Cast on 1 st.

Row 1: K 1, yo, k 1 in same st.

Row 2: K 1, yo, k 2.

Row 3: K 1, yo, k 3.

Row 4: K 1, yo, k across. Repeat row 4 until there are 52 sts on needle. Bind off (yo after the first st, sl first st over the yo).

Work 48 black triangles, 12 triangles of each of the 4 colors.

TO JOIN 2 TRIANGLES: Sew a black triangle to a color triangle, joining the bound-off edges.

TO MAKE PINWHEEL SQUARE: Alternating black with colors and always having the same color sequence for each square, join side edge of black triangle to side edge of next color triangle, weaving through edge sts.

Join 3 squares across and 4 squares in length.

BORDER: With black, work 2 rows of sc around afghan, working 3 sc in each corner st each row. Work 1 row of sl st around. End off.

Striped Afghan and Pillows

Garter stitch is used throughout for this attractive, functional afghan with pillows to match, in two closely related shades and white. Easy-to-handle panels are knit separately, then joined with single crochet.

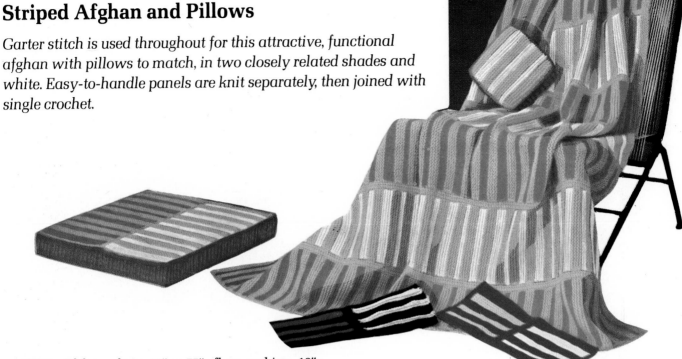

SIZE: Afghan, about 55″ x 75″; floor cushion, 18″ square; pillow, 7″ square.

MATERIALS: Knitting worsted, 10 4-oz. skeins light orange (A), 4 skeins dark orange (B), 3 skeins white (C) for afghan, one cushion and one pillow. Knitting needles No. 10. Steel crochet hook No. 0. Foam rubber, 2″ thick, 18″ square for cushion, 7″ square for pillow, or 2 squares, 1″ thick.

GAUGE: 4 sts = 1″; 8 rows = 1″.

Afghan:

FIRST PANEL (make 5): With A, cast on 28 sts. Work in garter st as follows: * 8 rows A, 4 rows B, 8 rows A, 6 rows B, 8 rows A, 8 rows B. Repeat from * until panel measures about 55″, ending with 8 rows A. With A, crochet 2 rows sc across each long edge, working 1 sc to each ridge (2 rows) of garter st.

SECOND PANEL (make 4): Work as for first panel but use C instead of B. With A, crochet 2 rows sc across each long edge.

FINISHING: With right sides tog, crochet panels tog as follows: With A, insert hook in first sc of first panel and in corresponding sc of second panel, draw lp through, complete as for sc, * insert hook in next sc on first panel and in corresponding sc on second panel, complete as for sc. Repeat from * across. Join all panels in this way, alternating A-B and A-C panels.

Floor Cushion:

Make two pieces same as first panel, each 16″ long. Make two pieces same as second panel, each 16″ long. Work 2 rows sc across each long edge as for afghan. Join two pieces same as afghan panels were joined. Repeat with other two pieces.

Boxing Strip: With B, cast on 10 sts. Work in garter st until strip is long enough, when stretched, to fit around four sides of cushion. Bind off. Sew ends of boxing strip tog. Place pieces over 18″ square foam rubber, stretching to fit, with boxing strip between. From right side, with B, join pieces to boxing strip with sc.

Pillow:

Work one piece same as first panel for 50 rows (one complete repeat plus 8 rows A). Work another piece same as second panel for 50 rows.

Boxing Strip: With B, cast on 10 sts. Work in garter st until strip is long enough, when stretched, to fit around four sides of pillow. Bind off. Sew ends of boxing strip tog. Place pieces over 7″ square foam rubber, stretching to fit, with boxing strip between. From right side, with B, join pieces to boxing strip with sc.

Quick-Knit Afghan

This easy-to-knit afghan is worked in two yarns: two strands of knitting worsted for the main color, one strand of bulky for contrast. The center panel and borders are knit in one piece; the side borders are picked up and knit in garter stitch. The details shown suggest other color combinations.

SIZE: About 48″ x 60″, plus fringe.

MATERIALS: Wool or Orlon of knitting-worsted weight, 11 4-oz. skeins main color (MC). Bulky wool or Orlon yarn, 9 2-oz. skeins contrasting color (CC). Two pairs of 18″ "jumper" knitting needles or 36″ circular needle No. 13. Aluminum crochet hook size K.

GAUGE: 3 sts = 1″; 11 rows = 2″ (pat).

Notes: Use double strand of knitting worsted (MC) and single strand of bulky yarn (CC) throughout afghan. If sts are too crowded on one 18″ needle, keep sts on two needles, knit with third and fourth needles. If circular needle is used, work back and forth on needle.

PATTERN (multiple of 2 sts): Sl all sl sts as if to purl.
Row 1 (right side): With CC, * k 1, yarn in back, sl 1, repeat from * across.

Row 2: With CC, * yarn in front, sl 1, yarn to back, k 1, repeat from * across.

Rows 3 and 4: With MC, knit.

Row 5: With CC, * yarn in back, sl 1, k 1, repeat from * across.

Row 6: With CC, * k 1, yarn in front, sl 1, yarn to back, repeat from * across.

Rows 7 and 8: With MC, knit. Repeat these 8 rows for pattern.

AFGHAN: With double strand MC, cast on 120 sts. Work in garter st (k each row) for 24 rows (12 ridges). Join single strand CC, work in pat until piece measures 56″ from start, end with row 2 of pat. Break off CC. With MC, work garter st for 24 rows (12 ridges). Bind off.

Side Border: From right side, with double strand MC, pick up and k 180 sts (about 3 sts to the inch) on one long side edge of afghan. Work in garter st for 24 rows (12 ridges). Bind off. Work border on other long side in same way.

FRINGE: Wind MC around 12″ cardboard; cut on one end. Hold 3 strands tog; fold in half. With crochet hook, draw folded lp through first st on side at lower edge of afghan, pull strands through lp and tighten. Knot fringe in st at other end of same row, then knot fringe in every other st between. Fringe top edge in same way. Trim evenly.

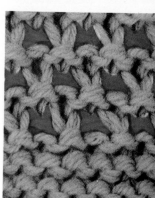

Box-Pattern Afghan

The blue box-pattern afghan is quick to knit on giant needles with four strands of knitting worsted. The easy-to-work pattern of stockinette and reverse stockinette squares makes the afghan reversible.

SIZE: 46" x 58", plus fringe.

MATERIALS: Knitting worsted, 14 4-oz. skeins. Jiffy knitting needles No. 35 (¾" diameter). Aluminum crochet hook size J.

GAUGE: 8 sts = 5"; 8 rows = 3¾" (4 strands of yarn tog).

PATTERN (multiple of 8 sts): **Rows 1-4:** * K 4, p 4, repeat from * across.

Rows 5-8: * P 4, k 4, repeat from * across. Repeat these 8 rows for pat.

Note: Work first and last sts of every row tightly.

AFGHAN: With 4 strands of yarn tog, cast on 72 sts evenly and snugly. Work row 1 of pat by knitting into back of sts to be knitted, purl the purl sts in usual way.

Continue in pat, working all sts in usual way after row 1, until 120 rows (15 pats) have been worked. Repeat rows 1-3. Bind off loosely in pat.

FINISHING: Stretch piece slightly in length to settle sts. With 2 strands of yarn tog, work 1 row sc around afghan, working 2 sc in each st on cast-on and bound-off edges, 2 sc in each knot on side edges, and 3 sc in each corner. Join with sl st in first sc. End off.

FRINGE: Wind yarn around 6" piece of cardboard. Cut yarn at one end (for 12" strands). Holding 4 strands tog, fold in half, draw loop through sc with crochet hook; draw ends through loop; tighten knot. Knot a fringe in every other sc around entire edge; knot a fringe in each of 3 sc at corners. Trim fringe evenly.

Cable Knit Afghan

Bold textured striping is formed by cables to make the yellow afghan shown at right. Two strands of sport yarn and two strands of knitting worsted are knit together as one on jumbo needles.

SIZE: 42" x 64", plus fringe.

MATERIALS: Knitting worsted, 7 4-oz. skeins yellow. Sport yarn, 7 2-oz. skeins yellow. Jumbo knitting needles No. 35 (¾" diameter). Large crochet hook.

GAUGE: 5 sts = 3"; 9 rows = 4" (4 strands tog, 2 strands of each yarn).

AFGHAN: Holding 2 strands of knitting worsted and 2 strands of sport yarn tog, cast on 69 sts. K 2 rows.

Pattern (multiple of 5 sts plus 4): **Row 1** (right side): K 1, * k 2nd st on left-hand needle but do not slip st off needle; k first st and slip both sts off needle (cable made), p 3. Repeat from * across to last 3 sts, work cable, k 1.

Row 2: K 1, * p 2, k 3, repeat from * across to last 3 sts, p 2, k 1.

Repeat these 2 rows for pat until afghan is 63" long, end right side. K 1 row on wrong side. Bind off in k on right side.

FINISHING: Wind yarn around 6" cardboard. Cut yarn at one edge (for 12" strands). Holding 2 strands of each yarn tog, fold strands in half; with crochet hook, pull loop through cast-on st, pull 8 ends through loop; tighten knot. Knot a fringe in each cast-on and bound-off st. Trim fringe evenly as desired.

Navajo Blanket

A Navajo blanket inspired this handsome afghan, knit all in one piece in stockinette stitch on a circular needle or long flexible knitting needles.

SIZE: 40" x 56", plus fringe.

MATERIALS: Knitting worsted, 5 4-oz. skeins royal blue (A); 4 skeins beige (B); 2 oz. each of light gold (C), medium gold (D), dark gold (E), orange (F), and scarlet (G). 29" circular knitting needle, or "jumper" needles, No. 8. Crochet hook size G. Twenty-four bobbins.

GAUGE: 5 sts = 1"; 13 rows = 2".

Notes: Use a separate bobbin for each color change. Always change colors on wrong side, picking up new strand from under dropped strand. Cut and join colors as necessary. Wind 5 bobbins A, 3 bobbins B; 4 bobbins each of C, D and E; 2 bobbins each of F and G.

AFGHAN: With A, cast on 200 sts. K 2 rows.

PATTERN: Row 1 (right side): P 1, k 1, p 1, * following chart, k from A to B, repeat from * once, end p 1, k 1, p 1.

Row 2: P 1, k 1, p 1, * p from A to B, repeat from * once, end p 1, k 1, p 1. Repeat rows 1 and 2 to top of chart (90 rows), then repeat chart 3 times more, repeat row 1. With A, k 1 row. Bind off in k, same tension as sts.

FINISHING: Run in yarn ends on wrong side. Steam-press lightly.

FRINGE: Cut A into 16" lengths. Hold 2 strands tog; fold in half. With crochet hook, draw folded lp through first st on end of afghan, pull strands through lp and tighten. Knot a fringe in each st on each end of afghan. Trim.

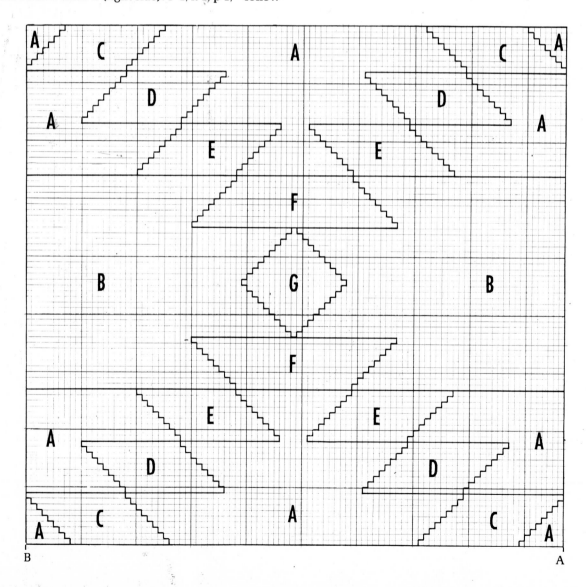

114

B

A

Flag Afghan

*The Continental flag inspired this distinctive knitted afghan.
Double knitting worsted, worked in stockinette stitch on a circular
needle, gives quick results. Felt stars are machine-stitched, sewn
on. Edges are fringed with gold yarn.*

SIZE: 42″ x 76″.

MATERIALS: Knitting worsted, 6 4-oz. skeins each of red and white, 4 skeins blue, 1 skein gold, 1 1-oz. skein black. Circular needle or long knitting needles size 13. Knitting needles size 10. Crochet hook size J. White felt, 72″ wide, ⅛ yd. White sewing thread.

GAUGE: 5 sts = 2″; 4 rows = 1″ (double strand of yarn). 4 sts = 1″ (single strand, size 10 needles).

Note: Flag is worked with double strand throughout.

FLAG: Beg at lower edge, with size 13 needles and double strand of red, cast on 180 sts. Work even in stockinette st (k 1 row, p 1 row) for 13 rows. * Change to white, work 13 rows. Change to red, work 13 rows. Repeat from * once, then change to white, work 13 rows; end p row.

Next Row: Change to red, k 90. Drop red. With blue, k 90.

Next Row: With blue, p 90; drop blue, pick up red from under blue strand to prevent hole, p 90. Continue with stripes of red and white at right half of flag, solid blue at left half, until 12 rows of 7th red stripe have been completed. Bind off in red and blue on next row.

FINISHING: Steam-press.

Band: With white and No. 10 needles, cast on 172 sts.

Row 1: P across.

Row 2: K 40. Join black. Working from row 1 of chart, k sts for letters in black, finish row with white.

Row 3: P 61 with white; reading from left to right on row 2 of chart, work next 71 sts from chart, p 40 white. Continue in this manner until top of chart is reached. Break off black. K 3 rows white (center k row forms ridge for folding band). Work even in stockinette st for 7 rows. Bind off. Steam-press band. Fold in half on ridge row. Sew ends closed. Place over left end of flag; sew in place.

With gold and crochet hook, work 1 row sc around bottom, right edge and top of flag, working 1 sc in each st at bottom and top, 1 sc in every other row at side edge and 3 sc in st at each corner. End off.

Cut gold in 6″ lengths. Holding 2 strands tog, knot a fringe in every sc around.

STARS: Using pattern for star, cut 13 stars from white felt. Machine-stitch each star as shown by lines on pattern. From paper, cut a circle 13″ in diameter. Pin to blue section of flag. Place stars around outer edge of circle, 2 points of each star touching circle; arrange stars as shown in illustration. Sew to flag with white thread.

Rose Afghan and Pillow

A cozy-warm afghan is embellished with roses for luxury. Diamonds, marked off with popcorn puffs, alternate in stockinette and reverse stockinette stitch. Twisted-spiral roses are embroidered in the challenging bullion stitch. The pillow front picks up the pattern; the back is plain.

AFGHAN: SIZE: 56″ x 48″, plus fringe.

MATERIALS: Orlon yarn of knitting-worsted weight, 15 4-oz. skeins winter white (W). For embroidery (afghan and pillow): 1 skein each of scarlet, blue, green. Knitting needles No. 13. Crochet hook size I. Tapestry needle.

GAUGE: 11 sts = 4″; 4 rows = 1″ (double strand of yarn).

Note: Popcorn: K very loosely in front and back of 1 st until there are 5 sts in 1 st, sl st worked in off left-hand needle, (with left-hand needle, pass 2nd st from tip of right-hand needle over and off needle) 4 times (1 st of group left).

Afghan:

Panels 1, 3 and 5: With double strand of W, cast on 29 sts. K 1 row, p 1 row.

Row 3 (right side): K 14, popcorn in next st (see Note), k 14.

Row 4: P 13, k 3, p 13.
Row 5: K 13, p 3, k 13.
Row 6: P 12, k 5, p 12.
Row 7: K 12, p 5, k 12.
Row 8: P 11, k 7, p 11.
Row 9: K 10, popcorn in next st, p 7, popcorn in next st, k 10.
Row 10: P 9, k 11, p 9.
Row 11: K 9, p 11, k 9.
Row 12: P 8, k 13, p 8.
Row 13: K 8, p 13, k 8.
Row 14: P 7, k 15, p 7.
Row 15: K 6, popcorn in next st, p 15, popcorn in next st, k 6.
Row 16: P 5, k 19, p 5.
Row 17: K 5, p 19, k 5.
Row 18: P 4, k 21, p 4.
Row 19: K 4, p 21, k 4.
Row 20: P 1, k 1, p 1, k 23, p 1, k 1, p 1.
Row 21: K 1, p 1, popcorn in next st, p 23, popcorn in next st, p 1, k 1.
Rows 22-39: Working back from row 20, work in pat to row 3. Repeat rows 4-39, 5 times more—6 diamonds in all. P 1 row, k 1 row. Bind off in p.

Panels 2 and 4: With double strand of W, cast on 23 sts. K 1 row, p 1 row.

Row 3 (right side): K 11, popcorn in next st, k 11.
Row 4: P 10, k 3, p 10.
Row 5: K 10, p 3, k 10.
Row 6: P 9, k 5, p 9.
Row 7: K 9, p 5, k 9.
Row 8: P 8, k 7, p 8.
Row 9: K 7, popcorn in next st, p 7, popcorn in next st, k 7.
Row 10: P 6, k 11, p 6.
Row 11: K 6, p 11, k 6.
Row 12: P 5, k 13, p 5.
Row 13: K 5, p 13, k 5.
Row 14: P 4, k 15, p 4.
Row 15: K 3, popcorn in next st, p 15, popcorn in next st, k 3.
Row 16: P 2, k 19, p 2.
Row 17: K 2, p 19, k 2.
Row 18: P 1, k 21, p 1.
Row 19: K 1, p 21, k 1.
Row 20: Knit.
Row 21: Purl.
Rows 22-39: Working back from row 20, work in pat to row 3. Repeat rows 4-39, 5 times more—6 diamonds in all. P 1 row, k 1 row. Bind off in p.

FINISHING: Steam-press panels. Embroider scarlet roses in center of purl diamonds as follows:

With double strand of scarlet, embroider 8 bullion stitches in a radiating circle. With single strand of green, embroider outline-stitch stems. With triple strand of green, embroider straight-stitch leaves (see stitch details, page 154). With backstitch, sew the 5 panels together in proper sequence, then embroider blue bullion-stitch roses as for scarlet roses in center of knit diamonds.

With double strand of W, work a row of sc on each long edge, keeping work flat.

FRINGE: Cut strands of W 22″ long. Using 6 strands for each fringe, pull through every 4th st on cast-on and bound-off edges. Knot ends of yarn close to edge of afghan. Trim.

Pillow:

SIZE: 20″ square.

MATERIALS: Orlon yarn of knitting-worsted weight, 2 4-oz. skeins winter white. Knitting needles No. 10. For embroidery see under afghan materials. 20″ square pillow form, or stuffing. Tapestry needle.

GAUGE: 15 sts = 4″; 11 rows = 2″.

PILLOW FRONT: Cast on 75 sts. K 1 row, p 1 row.

Row 3: K 13, popcorn in next st (see Note under Afghan), (k 23, popcorn in next st) twice, k 13.

Row 4: P 12, (k 3, p 21) twice, k 3, p 12.

Row 5: K 12, (p 3, k 21) twice, p 3, k 12.

Row 6: P 11, (k 5, p 19) twice, k 5, p 11.

Row 7: K 11, (p 5, k 19) twice, p 5, k 11.

Row 8: P 10, (k 7, p 17) twice, k 7, p 10.

Row 9: K 9, (popcorn in next st, p 7, popcorn in next st, k 15) twice, popcorn in next st, p 7, popcorn in next st, k 9.

Row 10: P 8, (k 11, p 13) twice, k 11, p 8.

Row 11: K 8, (p 11, k 13) twice, p 11, k 8.

Row 12: P 7, (k 13, p 11) twice, k 13, p 7.

Row 13: K 7, (p 13, k 11) twice, p 13, k 7.

Row 14: P 6, (k 15, p 9) twice, k 15, p 6.

Row 15: K 5, (popcorn in next st, p 15, popcorn in next st, k 7) twice, popcorn in next st, p 15, popcorn in next st, k 5.

Row 16: P 4, (k 19, p 5) twice, k 19, p 4.

Row 17: K 4, (p 19, k 5) twice, p 19, k 4.

Row 18: P 3 (k 21, p 3) 3 times.

Row 19: K 3 (p 21, k 3) 3 times.

Row 20: P 2, (k 23, p 1) twice, k 23, p 2.

Row 21: K 1, (popcorn in next st, p 23) 3 times, popcorn in next st, k 1.

Rows 22-39: Working back from row 20, work in pat to row 3. Repeat rows 4-39 twice more. P 1 row. Bind off.

BACK: Cast on 75 sts. Work in stockinette st (k 1 row, p 1 row) until piece measures same length as front. Bind off.

FINISHING: Steam-press to measure 20″ square. Embroider front as for afghan. Sew three sides, insert pillow (or stuffing), close fourth side.

Textured Stripes Afghan

Rich tones of gold, loden, melon, and orange are striped into blocks for a handsomely colorful afghan. The blocks are patterned in stockinette and slip stitches, then edged in crochet and sewn together in alternate fashion. Tassels add a final touch.

SIZE: About 64″ x 50″.

MATERIALS: Bulky acrylic yarn, 9 2-oz. skeins antique gold (G), 7 skeins loden (L), 6 skeins melon (M), 4 skeins orange (O). Knitting needles No. 15. Aluminum crochet hook size I. Large-eyed yarn needle.

GAUGE: Each square, blocked, measures 8½″.

Notes: Cut and join colors when necessary. Sl all sl sts as if to p.

SQUARES (make 32): With L, cast on 27 sts.

Row 1 (right side): Knit.

Row 2: Purl.

Rows 3 and 4: Repeat rows 1 and 2.

Row 5: With G, * k 1, yarn to back, sl 1, repeat from * across, end k 1.

Row 6: * K 1, yarn to front, sl 1, repeat from * across, end k 1.

Row 7: With M, * yarn to back, sl 1, k 1, repeat from * across, end sl 1.

Row 8: * Yarn to front, sl 1, k 1, repeat from * across, end sl 1.

Row 9: With G, knit.

Row 10: Repeat row 6.

Rows 11 and 12: With O, repeat rows 7 and 8.

Row 13: With G, repeat row 7.

Row 14: Repeat row 6.

Rows 15 and 16: With M, repeat rows 7 and 8.

Rows 17 and 18: Repeat rows 1 and 2.

Rows 19 and 20: With O, repeat rows 5 and 6.

Rows 21-24: Repeat rows 1-4.

Rows 25 and 26: With M, repeat rows 7 and 8.

Rows 27 and 28: Repeat rows 1 and 2.

Rows 29 and 30: With G, repeat rows 5 and 6.

Rows 31 and 32: With O, repeat rows 7 and 8.

Row 33: With G, repeat row 7.

Row 34: Repeat row 6.

Rows 35 and 36: With M, repeat rows 7 and 8.

Row 37: With G, knit.

Row 38: Repeat row 6.

Row 39: With L, repeat row 7.

Row 40: Purl.

Rows 41 and 42: Repeat rows 1 and 2. Bind off in knitting.

FINISHING: Weave in yarn ends. Steam-press pieces to 8½″ squares.

Join G with a sc in any corner. Ch 1, sc in same corner, * (ch 1, sc) 12 times across one edge to next corner, ch 1, (sc, ch 1, sc) in corner, repeat from * 3 times, end last repeat ch 1, sl st in first sc. End off. (See page 156 for general directions "To Crochet Edge on Knitting.")

From wrong side, weave squares together, alternating the direction of the squares, as pictured. The first row has 1 square, 2nd row, 3 squares, 3rd, 5 squares, 4th, 7 squares, 5th, 7 squares, 6th, 5 squares, 7th, 3 squares, 8th, 1 square. The edges are in a step sequence.

When all squares are sewn together, with M, work sc in every G sc around, having a ch 1 between sc's; at corners, work ch 2 between sc's.

FRINGE: Cut yarn 11″ long. Hold 4 strands of a color together; fold in half. With crochet hook, draw folded lp through ch-2 sp at a corner, pull strands through lp and tighten. Knot fringes around afghan as shown. Trim evenly. Steam-press afghan lightly.

Double-Knit Afghan and Pillows

A reversible afghan for the expert knitter! The double-knit pattern produces a honeycomb design on one side, a dotted effect on the other. The solid-color borders and lines are done in stockinette.

The blue-and-green pillows reveal the two sides of the double-knit pattern: the honeycomb side in green, the dotted side in blue. Make a pair of pillows to match your afghan.

SIZE: 46″ x 64″.
MATERIALS: Sports yarn, 9 2-oz. skeins each of gold (A) and black (B). 29″ circular needle No. 10.
GAUGE: 8 sts = 1″ (4 sts each side).

Afghan:

Border: With B, looping sts on needle with a single strand, cast on 358 sts. Join A.

Note: When knitting the k sts, hold both colors in back of work; when purling the p sts, hold both colors in front of work. Twist yarns tog at beg of every row for a firm edge.

Row 1 (Side A): * K 1 A, p 1 B, repeat from * across.

Row 2 (Side B): * K 1 B, p 1 A, repeat from * across. Repeat these 2 rows until border is 2″ from start, end row 2.

Narrow Stripe: Row 1 (Side A): (K 1 A, p 1 B) 10 times for side border, place a marker on needle, * k 1 B, p 1 A, repeat from * to last 20 sts, place a marker on needle, (k 1 A, p 1 B) 10 times for side border.

Note: Sl markers every row.

Row 2 (Side B): (K 1 B, p 1 A) 10 times for side border, * k 1 A, p 1 B, repeat from * across to marker, (k 1 B, p 1 A) 10 times for side border.

Row 3: Repeat row 1 of narrow stripe.

FIRST BLOCK PATTERN: Row 1 (Side B): Work border; (k 1 A, p 1 B) 3 times, * (k 1 B, p 1 A) 29 times, (k 1 A, p 1 B) twice, repeat from * 3 times more, (k 1 B, p 1 A) 29 times, (k 1 A, p 1 B) 3 times; work border.

Row 2 (Side A): Work border; (k 1 B, p 1 A) 3 times, † k 1 A, * (p 1 B, k 1 A) twice; skip first 2 sts on right-hand needle, insert left-hand needle in front of 3rd st and sl it over the 2 skipped sts and off needle (cluster), repeat from * 13 times more, p 1 B, (k 1 B, p 1 A) twice, repeat from † 3 times more, k 1 A, repeat from * to * 14 times, p 1 B, (k 1 B, p 1 A) 3 times more; work border.

Row 3 (Side B): Work border; (k 1 A, p 1 B) 3 times, † * k 1 B, p 1 A, k 1 B; with A, yo; passing next color to be used under the yo st, repeat from * 13 times, k 1 B, p 1 A, (k 1 A, p 1 B) twice, repeat from † 3 times, then repeat from * to * 14 times, k 1 B, p 1 A, (k 1 A, (k 1 A, p 1 B) 3 times; work border.

Row 4: Work border; (k 1 B, p 1 A) 3 times, † k 1 A, p 1 B, k 1 A, * (p 1 B, k 1 A) twice, work cluster as on row 2, repeat from * 12 times, p 1 B, k 1 A, p 1 B, (k 1 B, p 1 A) twice, repeat from † 3 times, k 1 A, p 1 B, k 1 A, repeat from * to * 13 times, p 1 B, k 1 A, p 1 B, (k 1 B, p 1 A) 3 times; work border.

Row 5: Work border; (k 1 A, p 1 B) 3 times, † k 1 B, p 1 A, * k 1 B, p 1 A, k 1 B; with A, yo; passing next color to be used under the yo st, repeat from * 12 times, (k 1 B, p 1 A) twice, (k 1 A, p 1 B) twice, repeat from † 3 times, k 1 B, p 1 A, then repeat from * to * 13 times, (k 1 A, p 1 B) twice, (k 1 A, p 1 B) 3 times; work border.

Repeat rows 2-5 7 times more, then repeat rows 2 and 3 once more, end on Side B. Repeat narrow stripe rows 1-3; end on Side A.

SECOND BLOCK PATTERN: Row 1 (Side B): Work border; (k 1 A, p 1 B) 3 times, * (k 1 B, p 1 A) 29 times, (k 1 A, p 1 B) twice, repeat from * 3 times more, (k 1 B, p 1 A) 29 times, (k 1 A, p 1 B) 3 times; work border.

Row 2 (Side A): Work border; (k 1 B, p 1 A) 3 times, * (k 1 A, p 1 B) 29 times, (k 1 B, p 1 A) twice, repeat from * 3 times more, (k 1 A, p 1 B) 29 times, (k 1 B, p 1 A) 3 times; work border.

Row 3: Work border; (k 1 A, p 1 B) 3 times, † k 1 B, * (p 1 A, k 1 B) twice, work a cluster, repeat from * 13 times, p 1 A, (k 1 A, p 1 B) twice, repeat from † 3 times, k 1 B, then repeat from * to * 14 times, p 1 A, (k 1 A, p 1 B) 3 times; work border.

Row 4: Work border; (k 1 B, p 1 A) 3 times, † * k 1 A, p 1 B, k 1 A; with B, yo, repeat from * 13 times, k 1 A, p 1 B, (k 1 B, p 1 A) twice, repeat from † 3 times, then repeat from * to * 14 times, k 1 A, p 1 B, (k 1 B, p 1 A) 3 times; work border.

Row 5: Work border; (k 1 A, p 1 B) 3 times, † k 1 B, p 1 A, k 1 B, * (p 1 A, k 1 B) twice, work a cluster, repeat from * 12 times, p 1 A, k 1 B, p 1 A, (k 1 A, p 1 B) twice, repeat from † 3 times, k 1 B, p 1 A, k 1 B, repeat from * to * 13 times, p 1 A, k 1 B, p 1 A, (k 1 A, p 1 B) 3 times; work border.

Row 6: Work border; (k 1 B, p 1 A) 3 times, † k 1 A, p 1 B, * k 1 A, p 1 B, k 1 A; with B, yo, repeat from * 12 times, (k 1 A, p 1 B) twice, (k 1 B, p 1 A) twice, repeat from † 3 times, k 1 A, p 1 B, repeat from * to * 13 times, (k 1 A, p 1 B) twice, (k 1 B, p 1 A) 3 times; work border.

Repeat rows 3-6 7 times more, then repeat rows 3 and 4 once more, end on Side A.

Narrow Stripe: Work rows 2, 1 and 2 of narrow stripe; end on Side B.

Next Row: Work border; (k 1 B, p 1 A) 3 times, * k 1 A, p 1 B, repeat from * across to last 26 sts, (k 1 B, p 1 A) 3 times; work border.

Repeat from first block pattern 3 times.

Border: Row 1 (Side B): * K 1 B, p 1 A, repeat from * across.

Row 2: * K 1 A, p 1 B, repeat from * across. Repeat these 2 rows until border matches border at other end. With B, bind off B sts, slipping A sts to a separate needle. Bind off A sts. Sew open edges tog.

FINISHING: Steam-press afghan using a steam iron or damp cloth and dry iron. If desired, using 2 strands of A or B, crochet 1 row of sl st around.

Double-Knit Pillows

SIZE: 16″ square.

MATERIALS: Knitting worsted, 4 ozs. each of Kelly green (A) and sapphire (B) for each pillow. 14″ knitting needles No. 10. Yarn needle.

GAUGE: 14 sts = 2″ (7 sts each side).

Note: Both pillows are made the same. One pillow uses Side A as right side, other pillow uses Side B.

PILLOW (make 2 pieces): With color A, looping sts on with single strand, cast on 114 sts. Join B.

Note: When knitting the k sts, hold both colors in back of work; when purling the p sts, hold both colors in front of work. Twist yarns tog at beg of rows for a firm edge.

Border: Row 1 (Side A): * K 1 A, p 1 B, repeat from * across.

Row 2 (Side B): * K 1 B, p 1 A, repeat from * across. Repeat these 2 rows until piece is 2″ from start, end row 2. Check gauge; piece should be 16″ wide.

Narrow Stripe: Row 1 (Side A): (K 1 A, p 1 B) 7 times for side border, place a marker on needle; * k 1 B, p 1 A, repeat from * across to last 14 sts, place a marker on needle; (k 1 A, p 1 B) 7 times.

Note: Sl markers every row.

Row 2 (Side B): (K 1 B, p 1 A) 7 times: * k 1 A, p 1 B, repeat from * to marker; (k 1 B, p 1 A) 7 times.

Row 3: Repeat row 1 of narrow stripe.

BLOCK PATTERN: Row 1 (Side B): Work border; (k 1 A, p 1 B) 3 times, * k 1 B, p 1 A, repeat from * to last 20 sts, (k 1 A, p 1 B) 3 times; work border.

Row 2 (Side A): Work border; (k 1 B, p 1 A) 3 times, k 1 A, * (p 1 B, k 1 A) twice; skip first 2 sts on right-hand needle, insert left-hand needle in front of 3rd st and sl it over the 2 skipped sts and off needle (cluster), repeat from * to last 21 sts, p 1 B, (k 1 B, p 1 A) 3 times; work border.

Row 3 (Side B): Work border; (k 1 A, p 1 B) 3 times, * k 1 B, p 1 A, k 1 B; with A, yo; passing B under the yo st, repeat from * to last 22 sts, k 1 B, p 1 A, (k 1 A, p 1 B) 3 times; work border.

Row 4 (Side A): Work border; (k 1 B, p 1 A) 3 times, k 1 A, p 1 B, k 1 A, * (p 1 B, k 1 A) twice, work cluster as on row 2, repeat from * to last 23 sts, p 1 B, k 1 A, p 1 B, (k 1 B, p 1 A) 3 times; work border.

Row 5 (Side B): Work border; (k 1 A, p 1 B) 3 times, k 1 B, p 1 A, * k 1 B, p 1 A, k 1 B; with A, yo; passing B under the yo st, repeat from * to last 24 sts, (k 1 B, p 1 A) twice, (k 1 A, p 1 B) 3 times; work border.

Repeat rows 2-5 10 times more, or until block pattern is square, end on Side B. Repeat narrow stripe rows 1-3, end on Side A. Beg on Side B, work border for 2″. Bind off on side to be used for right side by knitting 1 A and 1 B st tog with right-side color.

FINISHING: Steam-press pieces to 16″ squares. Sew three sides, insert pillow, close fourth side.

Aran-Stripe Afghan, Pillows and Bolster

Aran-Stripe Afghan

This luxurious afghan is striped with bold Aran patterns, worked up in five separate panels which are sewn together, bordered with garter stitch and then thickly fringed. Shown on page 126.

SIZE: 50″ x 62″.

MATERIALS: Orlon yarn of knitting-worsted weight, or Irish-type wool yarn, 13 4-oz. skeins. Straight knitting needles No. 8; 29″ circular needle No. 8. One dp needle for cables. Crochet hook size G.

GAUGE: 11 sts = 2″.

Note 1: Sl all sl sts as if to p.

Note 2: Twist St (tw-st): With dp needle, sl next st and hold in front of work, k next st, then k st for dp needle.

Note 3: Left Cable (l-cable): With dp needle, sl next 2 sts and hold in front of work, k next 2 sts. then k 2 sts from dp needle.

Note 4: Right Cable (r-cable): With dp needle, sl next 2 sts and hold in back of work, k next 2 sts, then k 2 sts from dp needle.

Note 5: Left Twist St (lt st): With dp needle, sl next 2 sts and hold in front of work, p next st, then k 2 sts from dp needle.

Note 6: Right Twist St (rt st): With dp needle, sl next p st and hold in back of work, k next 2 sts, then p st from dp needle.

Note 7: Cross Cable (cr-cable): With dp needle, sl next 3 sts and hold in back of work, k 2, then p 1, k 2 from dp needle.

Note 8: Popcorn: K loosely in front, back, front, back, front, back of next st (6 sts worked in 1 st), (with left-hand needle, pass 2nd st from tip of right-hand needle over and off needle) 5 times (1 st of group left).

Note 9: Left Cross St (lc st): With dp needle, sl next k st and hold in front of work, p next st, then k st from dp needle.

Note 10: Right Cross St (rc st): With dp needle, sl next p st and hold in back of work, k next st, then p st from dp needle.

PATTERN 1 (worked on 8 sts): **Row 1** (right side): R-cable on next 4 sts (see Note 4), l-cable on next 4 sts (see Note 3.)

Rows 2, 4 and 6: Purl.

Row 3: Knit.

Row 5: L-cable on next 4 sts, r-cable on next 4 sts.

Row 7: K 2, r-cable on next 4 sts, k 2.

Row 8: Purl. Repeat these 8 rows for pat 1.

PATTERN 2 (worked on 22 sts): **Row 1** (right side): P 9, l-cable on next 4 sts, p 9.

Row 2: K 9, p 4, k 9.

Row 3: P 8, rt st on next 3 sts (see Note 6), lt st on next 3 sts (see Note 5), p 8.

Row 4: K 8, p 2, k 2, p 2, k 8.

Row 5: P 7, rt st on next 3 sts, p 2, lt st on next 3 sts, p 7.

Row 6: K 7, p 2, k 4, p 2, k 7.

Row 7: P 6, rt st on next 3 sts, p 4, lt st on next 3 sts, p 6.

Row 8: K 6, (p 2, k 6) twice.

Row 9: P 5, (rt st on next 3 sts) twice, (lt st on next 3 sts) twice, p 5.

Row 10: K 5, p 2, k 1, p 2, k 2, p 2, k 1, p 2, k 5.

Row 11: P 4, (rt st on next 3 sts) twice, p 2, (lt st on next 3 sts) twice, p 4.

Row 12: (K 4, p 2, k 1, p 2) twice, k 4.

Row 13: P 4, k 1, lc st on next 2 sts (see Note 9), lt st on next 3 sts, p 2, rt st on next 3 sts, rc st on next 2 sts (see Note 10), k 1, p 4.

Row 14: K 4, (p 1, k 1) twice, p 2, k 2, p 2, (k 1, p 1) twice, k 4.

Row 15: P 4, k 1, p 1, lc st on next 2 sts, lt st on next 3 sts, rt st on next 3 sts, rc st on next 2 sts, p 1, k 1, p 4.

Row 16: K 4, p 1, k 2, p 1, k 1, p 4, k 1, p 1, k 2, p 1, k 4.

Row 17: P 4, lc st on next 2 sts, rc st on next 2 sts, p 1, l-cable on next 4 sts, p 1, lc st on next 2 sts, rc st on next 2 sts, p 4.

Row 18: K 5; with dp needle, sl next p st and hold in back, k next st, then k st from dp needle, k 2, p 4, k 2; with dp needle, sl next p st and hold in front, k next st, then k st from dp needle, k 5. Repeat rows 3-18 (16 rows) for pat 2.

PATTERN 3 (worked on 39 sts): **Row 1** (right side): P 5, cr-cable on next 5 sts (see Note 7), (p 7, cr-cable on next 5 sts) twice, p 5.

Row 2: K 5, (p 2, k 1, p 2, k 7) twice, p 2, k 1, p 2, k 5.

Row 3: P 4, rt st on next 3 sts, p 1, lt st on next 3 sts, (p 5, rt st on next 3 sts, p 1, lt st on next 3 sts) twice, p 4.

Row 4: K 4, p 2, k 3, p 2, (k 5, p 2, k 3, p 2) twice, k 4.

Row 5: P 3, (rt st on next 3 sts, p 3, lt st on next 3 sts, p 3) 3 times.

125

Aran-Stripe Afghan; inset: Fall Flower Pillow (TOP); Lattice Pattern Pillow (CENTER); and Irish Bolster (BOTTOM).

Row 6: K 3, (p 2, k 5, p 2, k 3) 3 times.

Row 7: P 2, (rt st on next 3 sts, p 5, lt st on next 3 sts, p 1) 3 times, p 1.

Row 8: K 2, p 2, k 7, (p 2, k 1, p 2, k 7) twice, p 2, k 2.

Row 9: P 2, k 2, p 3, popcorn in next st (see Note 8), p 3, (cr-cable on next 5 sts, p 3, popcorn in next st, p 3) twice, k 2, p 2.

Row 10: K 2, p 2, k 7, (p 2, k 1, p 2, k 7) twice, p 2, k 2.

Row 11: P 2, lt st on next 3 sts, p 5, rt st on next 3 sts, (p 1, lt st on next 3 sts, p 5, rt st on next 3 sts) twice, p 2.

Row 12: K 3, p 2, k 5, (p 2, k 3, p 2, k 5) twice, p 2, k 3.

Row 13: (P 3, lt st on next 3 sts, p 3, rt st on next 3 sts) 3 times, p 3.

Row 14: K 4, (p 2, k 3, p 2, k 5) twice, p 2, k 3, p 2, k 4.

Row 15: P 4, (lt st on next 3 sts, p 1, rt st on next 3 sts, p 5) twice, lt st on next 3 sts, p 1, rt st on next 3 sts, p 4.

Row 16: K 5, p 2, k 1, p 2, (k 7, p 2, k 1, p 2) twice, k 5.

Row 17: P 5, (cr-cable on next 5 sts, p 3, popcorn in next st, p 3) twice, cr-cable on next 5 sts, p 5.

Row 18: K 5, p 2, k 1, p 2, (k 7, p 2, k 1, p 2) twice, k 5. Repeat rows 3-18 (16 rows) for pat 3.

AFGHAN: PANEL 1 (right side panel): Beg at lower edge, with straight needles, cast on 52 sts. Beg on wrong side, work k 2, p 2, k 2, p 8, k 9, p 4, k 9, p 8, k 2, p 2, k 4. Mark end of last row for side edge.

Pattern: Row 1 (right side): K 4, tw-st on next 2 sts (see Note 2), p 2, work row 1 of pat 1 across next 8 sts, work row 1 of pat 2 across next 22 sts, work row 1 of pat 1 across next 8 sts, p 2, tw-st on next 2 sts, k 2.

Row 2: K 2, p 2, k 2, work row 2 of pat 1 across next 8 sts, work row 2 of pat 2 across next 22 sts, work row 2 of pat 1 across next 8 sts, k 2, p 2, k 4. Repeat last 2 rows, working and repeating the 8 rows of pat 1 and the 16 rows of pat 2 until pat 2 has been worked 23 times, end wrong side. Bind off in pat.

PANEL 2 (left side panel): Beg at lower edge, with straight needles, cast on 52 sts. Beg on wrong side, work k 4, p 2, k 2, p 8, k 9, p 4, k 9, p 8, k 2, p 2, k 2. Mark beg of last row for side edge.

Pattern: Row 1 (right side): K 2, tw-st on next 2 sts, p 2, work row 1 of pat 1 across next 8 sts, work row 1 of pat 2 across next 22 sts, work row 1 of pat 1 across next 8 sts, p 2, tw-st across next 2 sts, k 4.

Row 2: K 4, p 2, k 2, work row 2 of pat 1 across next 8 sts, work row 2 of pat 2 across next 22 sts, work row 2 of pat 1 across next 8 sts, k 2, p 2, k 2. Complete same as panel 1 (right side panel).

PANEL 3 (center panel): Beg at lower edge, with straight needles, cast on 50 sts. Beg on wrong side, work k 2, p 2, k 2, p 8, k 9, p 4, k 9, p 8, k 2, p 2, k 2.

Pattern: Row 1 (right side): K 2, tw-st on next 2 sts, p 2, work row 1 of pat 1 across next 8 sts, work row 1 of pat 2 across next 22 sts, work row 1 of pat 1 across next 8 sts, p 2, tw-st across next 2 sts, k 2.

Row 2: K 2, p 2, k 2, work row 2 of pat 1 across next 8 sts, work row 2 of pat 2 across next 22 sts, work row 2 of pat 1 across next 8 sts, k 2, p 2, k 2. Complete same as panel 1.

PANELS 4 AND 5 (center side panels): Beg at lower edge, with straight needles, cast on 65 sts. Beg on wrong side, work k 1, p 2, k 2, p 8, k 5, p 2, k 1, p 2, (k 7, p 2, k 1, p 2) twice, k 5, p 8, k 2, p 2, k 1.

Pattern: Row 1 (right side): K 1, tw-st on next 2 sts, p 2, work row 1 of pat 1 across next 8 sts, work row 1 of pat 3 across next 39 sts, work row 1 of pat 1 across next 8 sts, p 2, tw-st on next 2 sts, k 1.

Row 2: K 1, p 2, k 2, work row 2 of pat 1 across next 8 sts, work row 2 of pat 3 across next 39 sts, work row 2 of pat 1 across next 8 sts, k 2, p 2, k 1. Repeat last 2 rows, working and repeating the 8 rows of pat 1 and the 16 rows of pat 3 until pat 3 has been worked 23 times, omitting popcorns on row 17 of last pat 3 repeat, end wrong side. Bind off in pattern.

FINISHING: From wrong side, weave panels tog, matching rows.

Border: From right side, with circular needle, pick up and k 1 st in each st across cast-on edge of afghan. Working back and forth, work in garter st (k each row) for 3 rows. Bind off in k.

Work same border on bound-off edge of afghan.

FRINGE: Cut yarn into 15″ lengths. Hold 4 strands tog, fold in half; insert hook in first st on border, pull loop of yarn through, pull 8 ends through loop; tighten knot. Knot a fringe in every 3rd st across each border. Trim fringe evenly. Steam seams lightly on wrong side.

Fall Flower Pillow

Colorful embroidered flowers with an Alpine air spark an unusual square pillow. The knit diamonds are raised from a reverse stockinette background, separated by twisty stitches. Single crochet edges the fabric-backed pillow.

SIZE: 18″ square.

MATERIALS: Knitting worsted-weight yarn, 3 2-oz. balls natural. Knitting needles No. 8. One dp needle. Crochet hook size G. Tapestry wool, 1 10-yd. skein each of yellow (A), burnt orange (B), olive green (C) and rust (D). Sewing thread to match yarn. Pillow form 18″ square. Fabric to match yarn, ¾ yard. Tapestry needle.

GAUGE: 9 sts = 2″.

Note 1: Sl all sl sts as if to p.

Note 2: Left Purl St (l p-st): With dp needle, sl next st and hold in front of work, p next st, then k st from dp needle.

Note 3: Left Knit St (l k-st): With dp needle, sl next st and hold in front of work, k next st, then k st from dp needle.

Note 4: Right Purl St (r p-st): With dp needle, sl next st and hold in back of work, k next st, then p st from dp needle.

Note 5: Right Knit St (r k-st): With dp needle, sl next st and hold in back of work, k next st, then k st from dp needle.

PILLOW: Cast on 82 sts.

Row 1 (right side): K 1, p 4, * k 8, p 8, repeat from * across, end last repeat p 4, k 1.

Row 2: K 5, * sl 1 (see Note 1), p 6, sl 1, k 8, repeat from * across, end last repeat k 5.

Row 3: K 2, * p 3, l p-st on next 2 sts (see Note 2), k 4, r p-st on next 2 sts (see Note 4), p 3, k 2, repeat from * across.

Row 4: K 1, sl 1, * k 4, sl 1, p 4, sl 1, k 4, sl 2, repeat from * across, end last repeat sl 1, k 1.

Row 5: K 1, * l k-st on next 2 sts (see Note 3), p 3, l p-st on next 2 sts, k 2, r p-st on next 2 sts, p 3, r k-st on next 2 sts, repeat from * across, end k 1.

Row 6: K 1, p 1, * sl 1, k 4, sl 1, p 2, repeat from * across, end last repeat p 1, k 1.

Row 7: K 2, * l k-st on next 2 sts, p 3, l p-st on next 2 sts, r p-st on next 2 sts, p 3, r k-st on next 2 sts, k 2, repeat from * across.

Row 8: K 1, p 2, * sl 1, k 4, p 2, k 4, sl 1, p 4, repeat from * across, end last repeat p 2, k 1.

Row 9: K 3, * l k-st on next 2 sts, p 8, r k-st on next 2 sts, k 4, repeat from * across, end last repeat k 3.

Row 10: K 1, p 3, * sl 1, k 8, sl 1, p 6, repeat from * across, end last repeat p 3, k 1.

Row 11: K 5, * p 8, k 8, repeat from * across, end last repeat k 5.

Row 12: Repeat row 10.

Row 13: K 3, * r p-st on next 2 sts, p 3, k 2, p 3, l p-st on next 2 sts, k 4, repeat from * across, end last repeat k 3.

Row 14: K 1, p 2, * sl 1, k 4, sl 2, k 4, sl 1, p 4, repeat from * across, end last repeat p 2, k 1.

Row 15: K 2, * r p-st on next 2 sts, p 3, r k-st on next 2 sts, l k-st on next 2 sts, p 3, l p-st on next 2 sts, k 2, repeat from * across.

Row 16: K 1, p 1, * sl 1, k 4, sl 1, p 2, repeat from * across, end last repeat p 1, k 1.

Row 17: K 1, * r p-st on next 2 sts, p 3, r k-st on next 2 sts, k 2, l k-st on next 2 sts, p 3, l p-st on next 2 sts, repeat from * across, end k 1.

Row 18: K 1, p 1, * k 4, sl 1, p 4, sl 1, k 4, p 2, repeat from * across, end last repeat p 1, k 1.

Row 19: K 1, p 4, * r k-st on next 2 sts, k 4, l k-st on next 2 sts, p 8, repeat from * across, end last repeat p 4, k 1.

Row 20: Repeat row 2. Repeat rows 1-20 for pat 5 times more. Bind off in pat.

FINISHING: Block piece to measure 18" x 18". From right side, with crochet hook, work 1 rnd sc around pillow, working 3 sc in each corner and being careful to keep work flat.

Embroidery: Embroider 5 lazy daisy stitches (see pages 154-55) in center of each knit diamond, working each diagonal row of diamonds with another color as pictured.

Cut 19" square of backing fabric. Turn under ½" on all edges; sew to pillow top, inserting pillow form before closing last side.

Lattice Pattern Pillow

Popcorns and diamonds, drawn from Eire designs, center a stunning pillow. Seed and stockinette stitches, trimmed with crochet, are used for the rest.

SIZE: 15" x 19".

MATERIALS: Knitting worsted-weight yarn, 3 2-oz. balls natural. Knitting needles No. 8. One dp needle. Crochet hook size G. Fabric to match yarn for pillow back. Muslin, 1 yard for inner pillow. Dacron fiberfill. Sewing thread to match yarn.

GAUGE: 9 sts = 2".

Note 1: Sl all sl sts as if to p.

Note 2: Left Twist St (lt st): With dp needle, sl next 2 sts and hold in front of work, p 1, then k 2 from dp needle.

Note 3: Right Twist St (rt st): With dp needle, sl next st and hold in back of work, k next 2 sts, then p 1 from dp needle.

Note 4: Reverse Left Twist St (r-lt st): With dp needle, sl next 2 sts and hold in front of work, p next st, then sl 2nd sl st from dp needle back to left-hand needle and k it, then p 1 from dp needle.

Note 5: Reverse Right Twist St (r-rt st): With dp needle, sl next 2 sts and hold in back of work, p next st, then sl 2nd sl st from dp needle back to left-hand needle and k it, then p 1 from dp needle.

Note 6: Popcorn: (K 1, yo, k 1, yo, k 1) in next st, turn; k 5, turn; p 5; (with left-hand needle, pass 2nd st from tip of right-hand needle over and off needle) 4 times (1 st of group left).

Note 7: Seed Stitch Pat: Row 1: K 1, * p 1, k 1, repeat from * across. Repeat row, having k 1 over a p st and p 1 over a k st.

PILLOW: With No. 8 needles, cast on 81 sts.

Rows 1-12: Work in seed st pat (see Note 7).

Row 13: Work first 9 sts in seed st, k to within last 9 sts, finish row in seed st pat.

Row 14: Work first 9 sts in seed st, p to within last 9 sts, finish row in seed st pat.

Rows 15 and 16: Repeat rows 13 and 14.

Row 17: Work first 9 sts in seed st, k 4, * popcorn in next st (see Note 6), k 5, repeat from * 8 times, popcorn in next st, k 4, work last 9 sts in seed st pat.

Row 18 (wrong side): Work first 9 sts in seed st, p 6, * (k 1, p 1) 5 times, r-rt st (see Note 5) on next 3 sts, p 1, repeat from * twice, (k 1, p 1) 4 times, k 1, p 6, work last 9 sts in seed st.

Row 19: Work first 9 sts in seed st, k 4, lt st (see Note 2) on next 3 sts, (p 1, k 1) 3 times, p 1, rt st on next 3 sts, * k 1, lt st on next 3 sts, (p 1, k 1) 3 times, p 1, rt st on next 3 sts, repeat from * twice, k 4, work last 9 sts in seed st.

Rows 20, 22 and 24: Work first 9 sts in seed st, k all k sts and p all p sts to within last 9 sts, work last 9 sts in seed st.

Row 21: Work first 9 sts in seed st, k 5, lt st on next 3 sts, (p 1, k 1) twice, p 1, rt st on next 3 sts, k 1, * p 1, k 1, lt st on next 3 sts, (p 1, k 1) twice, p 1, rt st on next 3 sts, k 1, repeat from * twice, k 4, work last 9 sts in seed st.

Row 23: Work first 9 sts in seed st, k 4, p 1, k 1, lt st on next 3 sts, p 1, k 1, p 1, rt st on next 3 sts, k 1, p 1, * k 1, p 1, k 1, lt st on next 3 sts, p 1, k 1, p 1, rt st on next 3 sts, k 1, p 1, repeat from * twice, k 4, work last 9 sts in seed st.

Row 25: Work first 9 sts in seed st, k 4, popcorn in next st, p 1, k 1, lt st on next 3 sts, p 1, rt st on next 3 sts, * (k 1, p 1) 3 times, k 1, lt st on next 3 sts, p 1, rt st on next 3 sts, repeat from * twice, k 1, p 1, popcorn in next st, k 4, work last 9 sts in seed st.

Row 26: Work first 9 sts in seed st, p 4, (p 1, k 1) twice, * p 1, r-lt st on next 3 sts, (p 1, k 1) 5 times, repeat from * twice, p 1, r-lt st on next 3 sts, p 1, (k 1, p 1) twice, p 4, work last 9 sts in seed st.

Row 27: Work first 9 sts in seed st, k 4, p 1, k 1, p 1, rt st on next 3 sts, k 1, lt st on next 3 sts, * (p 1, k 1) 3 times, p 1, rt st on next 3 sts, k 1, lt st on next 3 sts, repeat from * twice, p 1, k 1, p 1, k 4, work last 9 sts in seed st.

Rows 28, 30 and 32: Work first 9 sts in seed st, k all k sts and p all p sts to within last 9 sts, work last 9 sts in seed st.

Row 29: Work first 9 sts in seed st, k 5, p 1, rt st on next 3 sts, k 1, p 1, k 1, lt st on next 3 sts, * (p 1, k 1) twice, p 1, rt st on next 3 sts, k 1, p 1, k 1, lt st on next 3 sts, repeat from * twice, p 1, k 5, work last 9 sts in seed st.

Row 31: Work first 9 sts in seed st, k 4, p 1, rt st on next 3 sts, (k 1, p 1) twice, k 1, lt st on next 3 sts, p 1, * k 1, p 1, rt st on next 3 sts, (k 1, p 1) twice, k 1, lt st on next 3 sts, p 1, repeat from * twice, k 4, work last 9 sts in seed st.

Row 33: Work first 9 sts in seed st, k 4, with dp needle, sl next st and hold in back of work, popcorn in next st, k next st, then p st from dp needle, * (k 1, p 1) 3 times, k 1, lt st on next 3 sts, p 1, rt st on next 3 sts, repeat from * twice, (k 1, p 1) 3 times, k 1; with dp needle, sl next 2 sts and hold in front of work, p 1, then k 1 from dp needle, popcorn in next st on dp needle, k 4, work last 9 sts in seed st. Repeat rows 18-33 twice, then repeat rows 18-32.

Next Row (right side): Work first 9 sts in seed st, k 4,

rt st on next 3 sts, (k 1, p 1) 3 times, k 1, lt st on next 3 sts, * p 1, rt st on next 3 sts, (k 1, p 1) 3 times, k 1, lt st on next 3 sts, repeat from * twice, k 4, work last 9 sts in seed sts.

Next Row: Repeat row 18.

Next Row: Repeat row 17.

Next Row: Repeat row 14.

Next Row: Repeat row 13. Repeat last 2 rows once. Work in seed st for 11 rows. Bind off in seed st.

FINISHING: Block piece to measure 15″ x 19″; do not flatten popcorns. From right side, with crochet hook, work 1 rnd sc around pillow, working 3 sc in each corner and being careful to keep work flat.

Cut two pieces of muslin 16″ x 20″; with right sides facing, sew tog with ½″ seams, leaving 3″ opening in center of one long edge. Stuff muslin pillow plumply. Sew opening closed. Cut 16″ x 20″ piece of backing fabric. Turn under ½″ on all edges; sew to pillow top, inserting muslin pillow before closing last side.

Irish Bolster

This fabulous Irish-inspired bolster is ringed with five different patterns. No question—the long pillow adds a most unusual decorative note!

SIZE: 25″ long, 7″ diameter.

MATERIALS: Yarn of knitting-worsted weight, 3 4-oz. skeins natural. Knitting needles No. 8. One dp needle. Crochet hook size G. Muslin, 1 yard for inner pillow. Dacron fiberfill. Sewing thread.

GAUGE: 9 sts = 2″.

Note 1: Sl all sl sts as if to p.

Note 2: Right Twist Purl St (rt p-st): With dp needle, sl next st and hold in back of work, k next 2 sts, then p 1 from dp needle.

Note 3: Left Twist Purl St (lt p-st): With dp needle, sl next 2 sts and hold in front of work, p next st, then k 2 from dp needle.

Note 4: Right Cross St (rc st): With dp needle, sl next 2 sts and hold in back of work, k 2, then k 2 sts from dp needle.

Note 5: Left Cross St (lc st): With dp needle, sl next 2 sts and hold in front of work, k next 2 sts, then k 2 sts from dp needle.

Note 6: Right Twist St (rt st): With dp needle, sl next st and hold in back of work, k next 2 sts, then k 1 from dp needle.

Note 7: Left Twist St (lt st): With dp needle, sl next 2 sts and hold in front of work, k next st, then k 2 sts from dp needle.

Note 8: Popcorn: (K 1, yo, k 1, yo, k 1) in next st, turn; k 5, turn; p 5; (with left-hand needle, pass 2nd st from tip of right-hand needle over and off needle) 4 times (1 st of group left).

PATTERN 1: Double Seed Stitch: Row 1: (wrong side): * K 2, p 2, repeat from * across.

Row 2: * P 2, k 2, repeat from * across.

Row 3: Repeat row 2.

Row 4: Repeat row 1. Repeat rows 1-4 for pat 1.

PATTERN 2: Row 1 (wrong side): P 2, k 6, p 2.

Row 2: Lt st (see Note 7) on next 3 sts, p 5, k 2.

Row 3 and All Odd Rows: P all p sts, and k all k sts.

Row 4: K 1, lt st on next 3 sts, p 4, k 2.

Row 6: K 2, lt p-st (see Note 3) on next 3 sts, p 3, k 2.

Row 8: K 2, p 1, lt p-st on next 3 sts, p 2, k 2.

Row 10: K 2, p 2, lt p-st on next 3 sts, p 1, k 2.

Row 12: K 2, p 3, lt p-st on next 3 sts, k 2.

Row 14: K 2, p 4, lt p-st on next 3 sts, k 1.

Row 16: K 2, p 5, lt p-st on next 3 sts. Repeat rows 1-16 for pat 2.

PATTERN 3: Row 1 (wrong side): Knit.

Row 2: Knit.

Row 3: Purl.

Row 4: Knit. Repeat rows 1-4 for pat 3.

PATTERN 4: Row 1 (wrong side): P 2, k 6, p 2.

Row 2: K 2, p 5, rt st (see Note 6) on next 3 sts.

Row 3 and All Odd Rows: P all p sts and k all k sts.

Row 4: K 2, p 4, rt st on next 3 sts, k 1.

Row 6: K 2, p 3, rt p-st (see Note 2) on next 3 sts, k 2.

Row 8: K 2, p 2, rt p-st on next 3 sts, p 1, k 2.

Row 10: K 2, p 1, rt p-st on next 3 sts, p 2, k 2.

Row 12: K 2, rt p-st on next 3 sts, p 3, k 2.

Row 14: K 1, rt p-st on next 3 sts, p 4, k 2.

Row 16: Rt p-st on next 3 sts, p 5, k 2. Repeat rows 1-16 for pat 4.

PATTERN 5: Row 1 (wrong side): K 2, p 2, (k 4, p 4) 3 times, k 4, p 2, k 2.

Row 2: P 2, (lt p-st on next 3 sts, p 2, rt p-st on next 3 sts) 4 times, p 2.

Row 3 and All Odd Rows: K all k sts and p all p sts.

Row 4: P 3, (lt p-st on next 3 sts, rt p-st on next 3 sts, p 2) 4 times, p 1.

Row 6: P 1, popcorn in next st (see Note 8), p 2, (rc st [see Note 4] on next 4 sts, p 4) 3 times, rc st on next 4 sts, p 2, popcorn in next st, p 1.

Row 8: P 3, (rt p-st on next 3 sts, lt p-st on next 3 sts, p 2) 4 times, p 1.

Row 10: K all k sts and p all p sts.

Row 12: P 3, (lt p-st on next 3 sts, rt p-st on next 3 sts, p 2) 4 times, p 1.

Row 14: P 1, popcorn in next st, p 2, (rc st on next 4 sts, p 4) 3 times, rc st on next 4 sts, p 2, popcorn in next st, p 1.

Row 16: P 3, (rt p-st on next 3 sts, lt p-st on next 3 sts, p 2) 4 times, p 1.

Row 18: P 2, (rt p-st on next 3 sts, p 2, lt p-st on next 3 sts) 4 times, p 2.

Row 20: P 1, rt p-st on next 3 sts, p 1, popcorn in next st, p 2, lc st (see Note 5) on next 4 sts, (p 4, lc st on next 4 sts) twice, p 2, popcorn in next st, p 1, lt p-st on next 3 sts, p 1.

Row 22: Rt p-st on next 3 sts, p 4, (rt p-st on next 3 sts, lt p-st on next 3 sts, p 2) 3 times, p 2, lt p-st on next 3 sts.

Row 24: Repeat row 10.

Row 26: Lt p-st on next 3 sts, p 4, (lt p-st on next 3 sts, rt p-st on next 3 sts, p 2) 3 times, p 2, rt p-st on next 3 sts.

Row 28: P 1, lt p-st on next 3 sts, p 1, popcorn in next st, p 2, lc st on next 4 sts, (p 4, lc st on next 4 sts) twice, p 2, popcorn in next st, p 1, rt p-st on next 3 sts, p 1. Repeat rows 1-28 for pat 5.

PILLOW: Cast on 112 sts.

Row 1 (wrong side): Work 8 sts in row 1 of pat 1, work next 10 sts in row 1 of pat 4, k 2, work next 6 sts in row 1 of pat 3, k 2, work next 10 sts in row 1 of pat 2, work next 36 sts in row 1 of pat 5, work next 10 sts in row 1 of pat 4, k 2, work next 6 sts in row 1 of pat 3, k 2, work next 10 sts in row 1 of pat 2, work last 8 sts in row 1 of pat 1.

Row 2: Work first 8 sts in row 2 of pat 1, work next 10 sts in row 2 of pat 2, p 2, work next 6 sts in row 2 of pat 3, p 2, work next 10 sts in row 2 of pat 4, work next 36 sts in row 2 of pat 5, work next 10 sts in row 2 of pat 2, p 2, work next 6 sts in row 2 of pat 3, p 2, work next 10 sts in row 2 of pat 4, work last 8 sts in row 2 of pat 1. Repeat last 2 rows, repeating the 4 rows of pat 1, 16 rows of pats 2 and 4, 4 rows of pat 3 and the 28 rows of pat 5 until piece measures 21" from start, end right side. Bind off in pat.

SIDE CIRCLES (make 2): Cast on 81 sts. P 1 row.

Row 2: (K 8, k 2 tog) 8 times, k 1—8 sts dec. P 1 row.

Row 4: (K 7, k 2 tog) 8 times, k 1—8 sts dec. P 1 row. Continue to dec 8 sts every other row, having 1 st less between decs until 17 sts remain, end p row.

Next Row: K 2 tog across, end k 1—9 sts. Cut yarn, leaving long end. Thread needle; draw remaining sts tog. Fasten securely on wrong side. Weave edges tog, forming circle.

FINISHING: Block pieces, being careful not to flatten pat. Cut muslin 26" x 22"; cut two 8" circles. With right sides facing, sew long edges of muslin tog, leaving 6" opening in middle. With right sides facing, sew a circle to each end of tube piece with ½" seams. Turn right side out; stuff plumply. Sl st opening closed.

Weave bound-off edge of pillow to cast-on edge, forming tube. From right side, with sc, crochet one circle to end of tube; join with a sl st in first sc. Do not turn. Working from left to right, sc in each sc around. Join; end off. Insert muslin pillow. Join 2nd circle to other end of tube same as first circle.

Lily Pond Afghan or Bedspread

An old and favorite bedspread motif, originally knitted in cotton, is adapted here in Orlon yarn for an afghan or a thick, warm bedspread. Small raised leaf motifs are sewn together to form the larger lily pond squares. Picture, page 132, courtesy of Bucilla Needlecraft.

SIZES: Directions for afghan about 52" x 73". Changes for bedspreads about 83" x 110" and 94" x 110", including fringe, are in parentheses.

MATERIALS: Sport yarn, 25 (59-66) 2-oz. balls (about 185 yards per ball). Knitting needles No. 6. Crochet hook size F.

GAUGE: Each small square should measure about 4½" before blocking.

SMALL SQUARE (make 96 [280-320]): Cast on 3 sts.

Row 1 (wrong side): Knit.

Row 2: Inc 1 st in first st, k 1, inc 1 st in last st—5 sts.

Row 3: K 1, p 3, k 1.

Row 4: Inc 1 st in first st, k 1, yo, k 1, yo, k 1, inc 1 st in last st—9 sts.

Row 5: K 2, p 5, k 2.

Row 6: Inc 1 st in first st, k 3, yo, k 1, yo, k 3, inc 1 st in last st—13 sts.

Row 7: K 3, p 7, k 3.

Row 8: Inc 1 st in first st, k 5, yo, k 1, yo, k 5, inc 1 st in last st—17 sts.

Row 9: K 4, p 9, k 4.

Row 10: Inc 1 st in first st, k 7, yo, k 1, yo, k 7, inc 1 st in last st—21 sts.

Row 11: K 5, p 11, k 5.

Row 12: Inc 1 st in first st, k 9, yo, k 1, yo, k 9, inc 1 st in last st—25 sts.

Row 13: K 6, p 13, k 6.

Row 14: Inc 1 st in first st, k 11, yo, k 1, yo, k 11, inc 1 st in last st—29 sts.

Row 15: K 7, p 15, k 7.

Row 16: Inc 1 st in first st, k 6, k 2 tog, k 11, sl 1, k 1, psso, k 6, inc 1 st in last st—29 sts.

Row 17: K 8, p 13, k 8.

Row 18: Inc 1 st in first st, k 7, k 2 tog, k 9, sl 1, k 1, psso, k 7, inc 1 st in last st—29 sts.

Row 19: K 9, p 11, k 9.

Row 20: Inc 1 st in first st, k 8, k 2 tog, k 7, sl 1, k 1, psso, k 8, inc 1 st in last st.

Row 21: K 10, p 9, k 10.

Row 22: Inc 1 st in first st, k 9, k 2 tog, k 5, sl 1, k 1, psso, k 9, inc 1 st in last st.

Row 23: K 11, p 7, k 11.

Row 24: Inc 1 st in first st, k 10, k 2 tog, k 3, sl 1, k 1, psso, k 10, inc 1 st in last st.

Row 25: K 12, p 5, k 12.

Row 26: Inc 1 st in first st, k 11, k 2 tog, k 1, sl 1, k 1, psso, k 11, inc 1 st in last st.

Row 27: K 13, p 3, k 13.

Row 28: Inc 1 st in first st, k 12, k next 3 sts tog, k 12, inc 1 st in last st—29 sts.

Row 29: Purl.

Row 30: K 1, * yo, k 2 tog, repeat from * to end—29 sts.

Row 31: Purl.

Row 32: Inc 1 st in first st, k to within 1 st of end, inc 1 st in last st—31 sts.

Row 33: Knit.

Row 34: Inc 1 st in first st, p to within 1 st of end, inc 1 st in last st—33 sts.

Row 35: Knit.

Row 36: K 2 tog, k to within 2 sts of end, k 2 tog—31 sts.

Row 37: Purl.

Row 38: K 2 tog, * k 2 tog, yo; repeat from * to within 3 sts of end, k 2 tog, k 1—29 sts.

Row 39: Purl.

Row 40: K 2 tog, k to within 2 sts of end, k 2 tog—27 sts.

Row 41: Knit.

Row 42: P 2 tog, p to within 2 sts of end, p 2 tog—25 sts.

Row 43: Knit.

Row 44: K 2 tog, k to within 2 sts of end, k 2 tog—23 sts.

Row 45: Purl.

Rows 46-61: Repeat rows 38-45 twice—7 sts.

Row 62: K 2 tog, k 2 tog, yo, k 2 tog, k 1—5 sts.

Row 63: Purl.

Row 64: K 2 tog, k 1, k 2 tog—3 sts. Bind off as to k.

FINISHING: Arrange 4 small squares to form a large square, as shown on chart. From right side, with care to have rows matching and seams elastic, sew from outer edge to center through knots at ends of adjacent rows. Close center by inserting needle under center st in first row of each petal and drawing tog. End off. Block large squares to 10½″ x 10½″ with care not to flatten petals and ridges.

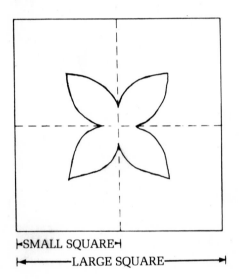

|◄SMALL SQUARE►|

|◄————————LARGE SQUARE————————►|

Arrange large squares as illustrated, having 4 (7-8) squares in width, 6 (10-10) squares in length. From right side, with care to have pats matching and to keep seams elastic, sew large squares tog. From right side, work 1 row sc around entire edge, with 3 sc in each corner; join with sl st in first st.

FRINGE: Wind yarn around an 11″ cardboard; cut at one end.

For Bedspread Only: Row 1: Knot a 6-strand fringe in upper right corner st and at each seam along both sides and lower edges only, with 6 6-strand fringes evenly spaced between, end with last fringe in upper left corner st, leaving entire upper edge unfringed.

Row 2: From right side, leaving 6 strands free, knot 6 strands of first fringe and 6 strands of 2nd fringe tog, about 1″ below first row of knots; knot remaining 6 strands of 2nd fringe and 6 strands of 3rd fringe tog, about 1″ below first row of knots; continue across, knotting 6 strands of last fringe and 6 strands of next fringe tog, having knots 1″ below and midway between knots of last row, end with last 6 strands free.

Row 3: From right side, knot first 6 free strands and 6 strands under first knot of last row tog, 1″ below last row of knots; knot remaining 6 strands under last knot of last row and 6 strands under next knot of last row, continue across, end by knotting remaining 6 strands under last knot and last 6 free strands tog.

Trim fringe evenly.

For Afghan: Work fringe in same manner as for bedspread on all 4 sides.

Lace Pattern Afghan

For knitters who love to work lace patterns, this lovely one-color afghan is the perfect choice. Knitted all in one piece, it features a vertical repeat design with solid and openwork patterns. The side edges are worked in garter stitch to keep the work flat. Make of knitting worsted or acrylic yarn of same weight.

SIZE: 50″ x 64″, plus fringe.

MATERIALS: Knitting worsted, 9 4-oz. skeins. 29″ circular knitting needles, size 10½.

GAUGE: 7 sts = 2″; 4 rows = 1″.

Note 1: Slip all sl sts as if to k.

Note 2: Twisted Rib Stitch (t-rb st): Slip next st, k 1 in front and back of next st, pass sl st over both sts on needle.

AFGHAN: Cast on 174 sts. Do not join.

Row 1 (right side): K 3, * yo, k 2 tog, repeat from * to within last 3 sts, k 3.

Row 2 and All Even Rows: K 3, p across to within last 3 sts, k 3.

Row 3: K 12, * (yo, k 2 tog) 4 times, yo, k 1, yo, k 3, sl 1 (see Note 1), k 1, psso, k 7, k 2 tog, k 3, (yo, k 2 tog) 4 times, k 9, * p 2 tog, yo, t-rb st on next 2 sts (see Note 2), yo, p 2 tog, k 9, repeat from first * once, then repeat between *'s once, k 3.

Row 5: K 12, * (yo, k 2 tog) 4 times, yo, k 3, yo, k 3, sl 1, k 1, psso, k 5, k 2 tog, k 3, (yo, k 2 tog) 4 times, k 9, * p 2 tog, yo, t-rb st on next 2 sts, yo, p 2 tog, k 9, repeat from first * once, then repeat between *'s once, k 3.

Row 7: K 12, * (yo, k 2 tog) 4 times, yo, k 5, yo, k 3, sl 1, k 1, psso, k 3, k 2 tog, k 3, (yo, k 2 tog) 4 times, k 9, * p 2 tog, yo, t-rb st on next 2 sts, yo, p 2 tog, k 9, repeat from first * once, then repeat between *'s once, k 3.

Row 9: K 12, * (yo, k 2 tog) 4 times, yo, k 7, yo, k 3, sl 1, k 1, psso, k 1, k 2 tog, k 3, (yo, k 2 tog) 4 times, k 9, * p 2 tog, yo, t-rb st on next 2 sts, yo, p 2 tog, k 9, repeat from first * once, then repeat between *'s once, k 3.

Row 11: K 12, * (k 2 tog, yo) 4 times, k 13, k 2 tog, k 3, yo, (k 2 tog, yo) 4 times, k 9, * p 2 tog, yo, t-rb st on next 2 sts, yo, p 2 tog, k 9, repeat from first * once, then repeat between *'s once, k 3.

Row 13: K 12, * (k 2 tog, yo) 4 times, k 3, sl 1, k 1, psso, k 7, k 2 tog, k 3, yo, k 1, yo, (k 2 tog, yo) 4 times, k 9, * p 2 tog, yo, t-rb st on next 2 sts, yo, p 2 tog, k 9, repeat from first * once, then repeat between *'s once, k 3.

Row 15: K 12, * (k 2 tog, yo) 4 times, k 3, sl 1, k 1, psso, k 5, k 2 tog, k 3, yo, k 3, yo, (k 2 tog, yo) 4 times, k 9, * p 2 tog, yo, t-rb st on next 2 sts, yo, p 2 tog, k 9, repeat from first * once, then repeat between *'s once, k 3.

Row 17: K 12, * (k 2 tog, yo) 4 times, k 3, sl 1, k 1, psso, k 3, k 2 tog, k 3, yo, k 5, yo, (k 2 tog, yo) 4 times, k 9, * p 2 tog, yo, t-rb st on next 2 sts, yo, p 2 tog, k 9, repeat from first * once, then repeat between *'s once, k 3.

Row 19: K 12, * (k 2 tog, yo) 4 times, k 3, sl 1, k 1, psso, k 1, k 2 tog, k 3, yo, k 7, yo, (k 2 tog, yo) 4 times, k 9, * p 2 tog, yo, t-rb st on next 2 sts, yo, p 2 tog, k 9, repeat from first * once, then repeat between *'s once, k 3.

Row 21: K 12, * (yo, k 2 tog) 4 times, yo, k 3, sl 1, k 1, psso, k 13, (yo, k 2 tog) 4 times, k 9, * p 2 tog, yo, t-rb st on next 2 sts, yo, p 2 tog, k 9, repeat from first * once, then repeat between *'s once, k 3.

Repeat rows 2 through 21 eleven times or until desired length, end row 9 or 21.

Next Row: Repeat row 2.

Next Row: Repeat row 1. Bind off.

FINISHING: Block.

FRINGE: Wrap yarn around a 14″ cardboard. Cut one end. Knot a fringe of 5 strands in each space on first and last rows. Trim ends.

Leaf Pattern Afghan

This elegant one-color knit afghan is worked all in one piece on a circular needle, alternating bands of double seed stitch with bands of raised leaf patterns. Picture courtesy of Bucilla Needlecraft.

SIZE: 48″ x 66″.

MATERIALS: Knitting worsted, 12 4-oz. skeins. Circular needle size 8, at least 24″ long.

GAUGE: 5 sts = 1″ (double seed st); 7 rows = 1″. 1 double seed st stripe plus 1 leaf stripe = 6″.

AFGHAN: Cast on 239 sts. Work back and forth on needle.

Double Seed St: Row 1 (wrong side): K 1, * p 1, k 1, repeat from * to end.

Row 2: K 1, * p 1, k 1, repeat from * to end.

Rows 3 and 4: P 1, * k 1, p 1, repeat from * to end. Repeat these 4 rows until 18 rows from beg, end on right side with pat row 2; **at the same time,** on last row place markers on needle between 15th and 16th sts from each end for beg and end of leaf pat. Carry markers.

Leaf Pat: Row 1 (wrong side): P 1, * k 1, p 1 *, repeat between *'s to marker; sl marker, k 209 to next marker, sl marker; p 1, repeat between *'s to end.

Row 2: P 1, * k 1, p 1 *, repeat between *'s to marker; sl marker; p 9, ** k 1, p 9, repeat from ** to next marker, sl marker; p 1, repeat between *'s to end.

Row 3: K 1, * p 1, k 1 *, repeat between *'s to marker; k 9, ** p 1, k 9, repeat from ** to next marker; k 1, repeat between *'s to end.

Row 4: K 1, * p 1, k 1 *, repeat between *'s to marker; p 9, ** yo, k 1, yo, p 9, repeat from ** to next marker; k 1, repeat between *'s to end—279 sts.

Note: Sts gained on rows 4, 6, 8 and 10 are lost on rows 12, 14, 16 and 18.

Row 5: Keeping borders in pat as established, work to marker; k 9, * p 3, k 9, repeat from * to marker; work border to end.

Row 6: Work border to marker; p 9, * k 1, yo, k 1, yo, k 1, p 9, repeat from * to marker; work border to end—319 sts.

Row 7: Work border to marker; k 9, * p 5, k 9, repeat from * to marker; work border to end.

Row 8: Work border to marker; p 9, * k 2, yo, k 1, yo, k 2, p 9, repeat from * to marker; work border to end—359 sts.

Row 9: Work border to marker; k 9, * p 7, k 9, repeat from * to marker; work border to end.

Row 10: Work border to marker; p 9, * k 3, yo, k 1, yo, k 3, p 9, repeat from * to marker; work border to end—399 sts.

Row 11: Work border to marker; k 9, * p 9, k 9, repeat from * to marker; work border to end.

Row 12: Work border to marker; p 9, * sl 1, k 1, psso, k 5, k 2 tog, p 9, repeat from * to marker; work border to end—359 sts.

Row 13: Same as row 9.

Row 14: Work border to marker; p 9, * sl 1, k 1, psso, k 3, k 2 tog, p 9, repeat from * to marker; work border to end—319 sts.

Row 15: Same as row 7.

Row 16: Work border to marker; p 9, * sl 1, k 1, psso, k 1, k 2 tog, k 9, repeat from * to marker, work border to end—279 sts.

Row 17: Same as row 5.

Row 18: Work border to marker; p 9, * sl 1, k 2 tog, pass sl st over the k 2 tog, p 9, repeat from * to marker; work border to end—239 sts.

Row 19: Work border to marker; k 209; work border to end.

Row 20: Work border to marker; p 209; work border to end.

Beg with row 3, work double seed st for 18 rows. Keeping borders in pat as established, continue to alternate 20 rows of leaf pat and 18 rows of double seed st until 11 double seed st stripes and 10 leaf pat stripes have been completed. Bind off in pat.

FINISHING: Block to given measurements.

FRINGE: Wind yarn around a 10″ cardboard. Cut at one end. Knot 40 10-strand fringes evenly spaced along cast-on and bound-off edges.

IV Special Techniques

Hairpin Lace Afghan

Hairpin lace panels are joined together in pairs by means of fill-in strips worked in a raised popcorn pattern. Nine popcorn panels with hairpin lace loops on both edges are looped together.

SIZE: 54″ x 66″, plus fringe.

MATERIALS: Yarn of knitting-worsted weight, 13 4-oz. skeins blue. 2″ hairpin lace crochet loom. Crochet hook size E.

GAUGE: 1 panel (2 hairpin lace strips with crochet fill-in) = 6″; 5 crochet rows = 3″.

AFGHAN: PANEL (make 9): For each panel, make 2 strips of hairpin lace on 2″ wide loom, having 333 loops on each side of each strip. (See page 142.)

Crochet Fill-in: Make lp on hook; insert hook through first 3 loops on right-hand edge of first hairpin lace strip, make 1 sc, ch 14, sc tog first 3 loops of 2nd hairpin lace strip, ch 2; insert hook in next 3 loops of 2nd hairpin lace strip, yo and through all 4 loops on hook. Ch 1, turn.

Row 1: Dc in first ch of ch 14, ch 2, sk 2 ch, 5 dc in next ch, drop loop off hook, insert hook through top of first dc, pick up dropped loop and pull through st (popcorn made); (ch 2, sk 2 ch, popcorn in next ch) twice, ch 2, sk 2 ch, dc in next ch, yo hook, draw up a loop in last ch, yo and through 2 loops on hook, insert hook in next 3 loops on first hairpin lace strip, yo and through all 5 loops, ch 2, insert hook in next 3 loops of hairpin lace strip, yo and through 4 loops on hook. Ch 1, turn.

Row 2: Dc in next dc, dc in ch-2 sp, (ch 2, 2 dc in next ch-2 sp) twice, ch 2, dc in next ch-2 sp, dc in next dc, yo hook, draw up a loop in top of ch 2, yo and through 2 loops, insert hook through next 3 loops of hairpin lace strip, yo and through all 5 loops. Ch 2, insert hook through next 3 loops of hairpin lace, yo and through all 4 loops. Ch 1, turn.

Row 3: Dc in next dc, (ch 2, popcorn in next ch-2 sp) 3 times, ch 2, sk 1 dc, dc in next dc, yo, draw up a loop in top of ch 2, yo and through 2 loops, insert hook in next 3 loops of hairpin lace, yo and through all 5 loops on hook. Ch 2, insert hook in next 3 loops of hairpin lace, yo and through all 4 loops on hook. Ch 1, turn.

Repeat rows 2 and 3 until all loops of hairpin lace have been joined.

TO JOIN PANELS: Insert hook through first 3 loops on one panel, pick up first 3 loops on next panel and pull them through loops on hook, * pick up next 3 loops on first panel and pull them through, pick up next 3 loops on next panel and pull them through, repeat from * to top. Tack top loops tog.

FRINGE: Cut yarn in 12″ lengths. Using 2 strands tog for each fringe, knot fringe closely across top and bottom of afghan.

HOW TO MAKE HAIRPIN LACE

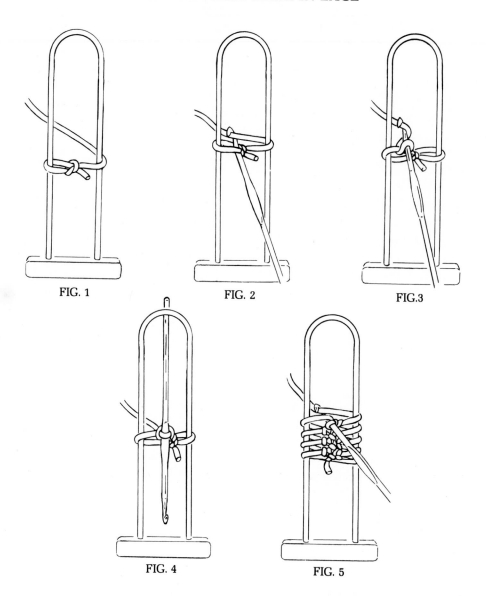

FIG. 1   FIG. 2   FIG.3

FIG. 4   FIG. 5

Use a crochet hook and a hairpin lace loom. Width of hairpin lace depends on the size of hairpin loom used. This loom is sometimes called a fork or staple.

With crochet hook, make a loose chain stitch. Take hook out of stitch and insert left-hand prong of loom through chain stitch. Draw out ch (loop) until knot is halfway between prongs. Then bring thread to front and around right-hand prong to back (Fig. 1). Insert crochet hook up through loop on left-hand prong, draw thread through and make a chain (Figs. 2 and 3). * To get crochet hook in position for next step, without drawing out loop on hook, turn handle of crochet hook upward parallel with prongs, then pass it through the prongs to back of loom (Fig. 4). Now turn loom toward you from right to left once (a loop over right prong). With a loop on hook, insert crochet hook up through loop on left-hand prong, in back of front thread, draw thread through (Fig. 5) and complete single crochet. Repeat from *

Note: Some prefer to withdraw crochet hook from loop, turn loom over as directed and reinsert hook, instead of method illustrated in Fig. 4.

When loom gets crowded, remove base, slide most of loops off, leaving last few on and replace base.

Jigsaw Puzzle Afghan

A fantastic and whimsical afghan, this jigsaw puzzle of crocheted motifs cannot be duplicated. Although it is impossible to give specific directions for making the afghan, some suggestions for designing your own are useful. Shown on page 144.

SIZE: Usual size for an afghan is 40″ to 50″ wide and 60″ to 80″ long. Your afghan can be any size, depending on the size and number of motifs you make.

MATERIALS: Use all your leftover yarns of knitting-worsted weight. Lighter-weight yarns can be used double. Variegated yarns are useful for filling in between motifs, for making floral motifs, and for working the border. Novelty yarns such as angora, mohair, metallic yarns, and tweeds could be used for special effects on some motifs. A size G hook is a good average size to use, but you can vary the hook size on different motifs.

MOTIFS: The afghan shown will suggest many suitable ideas. These are some of the motifs used:

Food: Lemon meringue pie slice, watermelon slice, ice cream soda, ice cream cone.

Animal and Plant Life: Cat, fish, elephant (with flappable ear), grapes, leaves, flowers, worm.

Other Motifs: Hand, heart, LOVE, brown jug, smiling face, eight ball, stop sign, key.

After working a motif, crochet around it with 1 or more rows of single crochet or double crochet in contrasting colors to make motif larger.

Make a number of nonobjective motifs: squares, circles, semicircles, ovals, triangles, rectangles, hexagons.

FINISHING: Arrange motifs on a plain sheet. Baste in position about 1″ in from edge of motif. Make additional motifs as needed to fill in big spaces. Sew motifs tog along all edges that touch with matching yarn. Fill in spaces between motifs with rows of stitches graduating in size as needed to fill spaces. Sew all touching edges tog. Fill out spaces around four sides to make even edges. Work border around afghan in rounds of single crochet or double crochet, working 3 sts in each corner of each round to keep corners flat.

Broomstick Lace Afghan

Broomstick lace offers you a quick way to make an afghan. Yarn is looped over a thick knitting needle, then worked off in groups with single crochet. Use six colors as shown, one predominant, or choose a rainbow of colors. Picture courtesy Bucilla Needlecraft.

SIZE: 42" x 67", including fringe.

MATERIALS: Yarn of knitting-worsted weight (about 180 yards per skein), 6 2-oz. skeins A; 2 skeins each of B and C; 1 skein each of D, E, and F. One knitting pin, size 50. Crochet hook size K.

GAUGE: 5 pats = 5½"; 10 pats = 11"; 7 rows = 9".

SWATCH FOR CHECKING GAUGE: Row 1: First Half: See Figures 1 and 2. Ch 25, sl lp on hook to needle; holding needle in left hand, working from left to right on ch, * insert hook in next ch, draw lp through, and with care not to twist, sl this lp on needle, repeat from * to end—25 lps.

2nd Half of Row: See Figures 3 and 4. Insert hook from right to left through first 5 lps on needle (1 group), draw yarn through with care not to tighten first lp, ch 1 at top of group and sl from needle, work 5 sc in center sp of group; * insert hook through next 5 lps on needle, yo and through these 5 lps, sl them from needle, yo and through 2 lps on hook for first sc, work 4 more sc in center sp of group, repeat from * to end—25 sc; 5 pats.

Row 2: First Half: See Figures 5 and 6. Do not turn. Sl lp from hook on to needle; * working from left to right, insert hook under back lp only of next sc, draw lp through, and with care not to twist, sl this lp onto needle; repeat from * to end—25 lps.

2nd Half: Same as 2nd half of row 1. Repeat row 2 for pat until 8 rows from beg. End off.

Block to about 5¾" wide x 7" long. **Note:** If swatch is too wide, use smaller hook to tighten gauge; if swatch is too narrow, loosen work.

AFGHAN: With A, ch 190 for lower edge.

Row 1: Work first half of row same as first half of row for swatch—190 lps on needle. Work 2nd half of row same as 2nd half of row for swatch—38 pats. Fasten off A. **Note:** Fasten off at end of each full row. Do not turn.

Beg in each succeeding row by drawing lp of next color through back lp of first sc and sl it to pin. Work in back lp only of all sc. * Work 1 row each B, A, C, A, D, A, E, A, F, A, repeat from * 3 times—41 rows. Work 1 row each B, A, C, A.

FINISHING: Block to 42" x 57".

FRINGE: Wind A around an 8" cardboard. Cut at one end. Knot a 4-strand fringe at corners and in spaces between pats on upper and lower edges. Trim.

HOW TO MAKE BROOMSTICK LACE

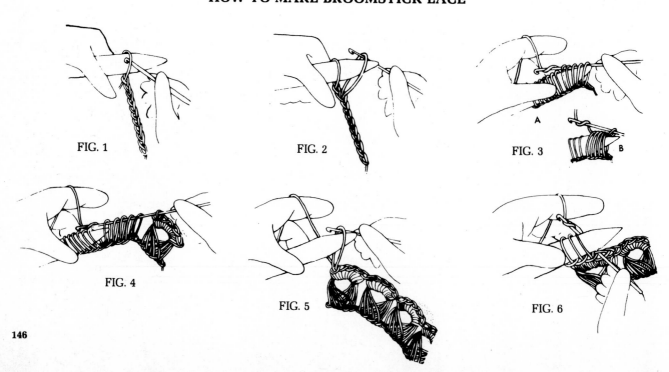

FIG. 1

FIG. 2

FIG. 3

FIG. 4

FIG. 5

FIG. 6

Daisy Afghan

Daisies that make up this lacy coverlet are formed on a loom and crocheted together with a picot edging. For variety, make flowers of many colors, or use one color for all daisies, another color for background.

SIZE: 48" x 70".

MATERIALS: Yarn of knitting-worsted weight, 17 2-oz. skeins (about 180 yards per skein). Daisy Winder. Steel crochet hook No. 2. Tapestry needle.

GAUGE: 1 daisy = 2" (with edge).

Follow directions given with Daisy Winder. Make 782 daisies with 12 double petals. Afghan has 34 rows of 23 daisies.

AFGHAN: Note: Join daisies on right side, working in double lps of each of 12 petals. **Row 1:** With yarn, make lp on crochet hook, sc in lps at end of a daisy petal; do not twist petals; * (ch 2, sc) in each of next 3 petals; **for free picot,** ch 5, sl st in front and side lp of last sc, repeat from * once, (ch 2, sc) in 8th and 9th petals; sc in petal of a new daisy, ch 2, sc in next petal of new daisy; **for sl-st joining,** drop lp off hook, insert hook in sc of 8th petal of last daisy and pull dropped lp through, ** ch 2, sc in 3rd petal of new daisy; **for picot-joining,** ch 2, drop lp off hook, insert hook in center ch of p (picot) of last daisy and pull dropped lp through, ch 2, sl st in front and side lp of last sc of new daisy to complete picot-joining; (ch 2, sc) in each of next 3 petals of new daisy, make free p, (ch 2, sc) in each of 7th and 8th petals of new daisy †; sc in petal of a new daisy, ch 2, sc in next petal of new daisy, make sl-st joining as before in 7th petal of last daisy (first and 2nd petals of new daisy joined to 8th and 7th petals of last daisy) **. Repeat from ** to 2nd ** until 23 daisies are joined, end at †. Do not end off. Work as follows.

Complete Edge on Free Petals: Ch 2, sc in 9th petal, make free p as before, * (ch 2, sc) in each of next 3 free petals, make free p, ch 2, make sl-st joining in top of joining-st between last and next daisy, ch 2, sc in next free petal, make picot-joining in center ch of last p of last daisy, repeat from * across, ending in 10th petal of 23rd daisy; (ch 2, sc) in each of 11th and 12th petals, ch 2, sl st in sc of first petal, make free p. End off. Mark last p starting point for following daisy rows.

Row 2: Make lp on hook, sc in petal end of a new daisy, (ch 2, sc) in each of next 3 petals; working from right to left across last worked edge of last row, make picot-joining in center ch of marked p, * (ch 2, sc in next petal of new daisy, make sl-st joining in sc of next petal of daisy on last row) twice, ch 2, sc in new petal of new daisy †, make picot-joining in center of the 2 joined p on last row, (ch 2, sc) in each of next 2 petals of new daisy; sc in petal of a new daisy, ch 2, sc in 2nd petal of new daisy, make sl-st joining in sc of 2nd from last joined petal of last daisy of new row, ch 2, sc in 3rd petal of new daisy, make picot-joining in center of the 3 joined p, repeat from * until 23 daisies are joined, end at †, make picot-joining in center ch of free p on last row, (ch 2, sc) in each of 7th and 8th petals of new daisy. Do not end off. Complete edge of free petals as for row 1. Repeat row 2 until 34 rows of 23 daisies are joined.

BORDER: Make lp on hook, from right side, † work sc in 2nd ch-2 sp to left of free corner p, * make p of ch 3 in sc last worked, ch 2, sc in next ch-2 sp, ch 2, sc and p of ch 3 in joining-st between next 2 p, (ch 2, sc) in each of next 2 ch-2 sps of next daisy, repeat from * to within 1 ch-2 sp of next corner; make p of ch 3 in sc last worked, ch 2, sc in next ch-2 sp, ch 2, sc and p of ch 3 in center ch of corner p, ch 2, sc in next ch-2 sp, ch 2, repeat from †, 3 times. Join with sl st in first sc. End off. Run in ends on wrong side.

Steam-press afghan lightly, stretching slightly to 48" x 70", using steam iron or damp cloth and dry iron.

Rosette Afghan and Pompon Pillow

This easy-to-work afghan combines narrow strips of square rosettes, made on a loom, and wider strips of crocheted loops. The sides are picot-edged, ends are fringed. The pillow cover is knitted in a lacy drop-stitch pattern, and fits over a 14" round pillow form. Add a pompon in contrasting color.

Afghan:

SIZE: 48" x 60", plus fringe.

MATERIALS: Knitting worsted, 10 4-oz skeins. Plastic crochet hook, size 5 or F. Tool for making 2" square rosettes. Yarn needles.

GAUGE: 1 rosette with edging = 2½" square; 3 chain loops = 2"; 2 rows = 1".

FLOWER PANELS (make 4): Using flower maker, make 52 square motifs with double petals for each panel, following directions that come with tool. Do not finish edges. Remove from tool. Make lp on hook, sc in end of double petal at one corner. * Ch 4, sc in next double petal, ch 3, sc in next double petal, ch 4, sc in next corner petal. Repeat from * around, join with sl st in first sc. End off. Pull corners to square rosette.

To join rosettes, place right sides of two tog. Thread yarn in large-eyed needle. Whip rosettes tog along one edge, matching stitches, sewing through top lp of each st. Join rosettes in a panel two rosettes wide by 26 rosettes long.

CHAIN-LOOP PANELS: Narrow Panel (make 2): Ch 23. **Row 1:** Sc in 7th ch from hook, * ch 4, sk 3 ch, sc in next ch, repeat from * across—5 loops. Ch 5, turn.

Row 2: Sc in first loop, * ch 4, sc in next loop, repeat from * across—5 loops. Ch 5, turn. Repeat row 2 until piece is same length as flower panel.

Wide Panel (make 3): Ch 47. Work as for narrow panel—11 loops.

FINISHING: Alternate chain-loop panels and flower panels, having narrow panels at sides, all chain loops in one direction and all rosettes face up. Whip panels tog from wrong side.

Crocheted Edging: From right side, join yarn in first loop on side edge of afghan, sc in same loop, ch 3, sl st in same loop, * sc in sc at end of next row, ch 3, sl st in same sc (picot), sc in end loop of next row, repeat from * across side of afghan. End off. Repeat on other side.

FRINGE: Cut yarn in 5" lengths. Hold two tog; fold in half. Put folded end through chain loop at bottom edge of afghan; pull ends through folded loop. Knot fringe in this manner across bottom and top of afghan, making 3 fringe knots in each chain loop. Trim fringe.

Round Pompon Pillow:

MATERIALS: Sport yarn, 1 2-oz. skein. Knitting worsted for pompon, 1 oz. contrasting color. Knitting needles No. 5. Foam rubber pillow form, 14" round with 2" boxing. Fabric for covering pillow, ½ yard. Matching sewing thread. One button, ¾" diameter, with 2 holes. Button thread. Upholstery and tapestry needles.

PILLOW TOP: With sport yarn, cast on 30 sts. **Row 1:** Knit.

Row 2: K 6, (yo, k 1) 6 times, (yo twice, k 1) 6 times, (yo 3 times, k 1) 6 times, (yo 4 times, k 1) 6 times (outer edge).

Row 3: K each st, drop all extra windings off left needle—30 sts.

Row 4: Knit. Repeat rows 1-4 until outer edge, when stretched, fits around outer edge of pillow (about 44"), end row 3. Bind off loosely. Sew bound-off edge to cast-on edge. Thread double strand of yarn in tapestry needle, run through inner edge of pillow top; gather sts tog.

POMPON: Wind knitting worsted about 200 times around a 3" cardboard. Tie strands tightly tog at one edge with double strand of button thread. Cut through strands at opposite edge of cardboard. Trim pompon.

FINISHING: Cover pillow form with fabric. Fit pillow top over pillow, bringing outer edge down over boxing to back edge of pillow. Sew in place around edge. Thread upholstery needle with double strand of button thread. Secure end to back of pompon, stitching through pompon several times. Insert needle through center top of pillow to back, stitch through holes of button, come back through pillow; pull thread tightly to dimple pillow at center. Stitch through pompon; end off.

V Abbreviations, Stitches and Additional How-To's

Abbreviations

Knitting Abbreviations

k—knit
p—purl
st—stitch
sts—stitches
yo—yarn over
sl—slip
sk—skip
tog—together
rnd—round

psso—pass slip stitch over
inc—increase
dec—decrease
beg—beginning
pat—pattern
lp—loop
MC—main color
CC—contrasting color
dp—double-pointed

Crochet Abbreviations

ch—chain stitch
st—stitch
sts—stitches
lp—loop
inc—increase
dec—decrease
rnd—round
beg—beginning
sk—skip
p—picot
tog—together
sc—single crochet

sl st—slip stitch
dc—double crochet
hdc—half double crochet
tr—treble, or triple, crochet
dtr—double treble crochet
tr tr—treble treble crochet
bl—block
sp—space
cl—cluster
pat—pattern
yo—yarn over hook

How to Follow Directions

An asterisk (*) is often used in crochet directions to indicate repetition. For example, when directions read " * 2 dc in next st, 1 dc in next st, repeat from * 4 times" this means to work directions after first * until second * is reached, then go back to first * 4 times more. Work 5 times in all.

When ( ) (parentheses) are used to show repetition, work directions within parentheses as many times as specified. For example, " (dc, ch 1) 3 times" means to do what is within ( ) 3 times altogether.

"Work even" in directions means to work the same stitch without increasing or decreasing.

Stitches

Embroidery Stitches

SATIN STITCH

STRAIGHT STITCH

BACKSTITCH

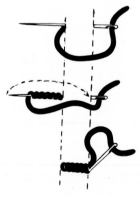

BULLION STITCH

FRENCH KNOT

CHAIN STITCH

OUTLINE STITCH

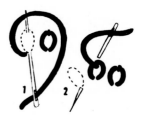

LAZY DAISY STITCH

Plain Afghan Stitch

FIG. 1

FIG. 2

FIG. 3

FIG. 4

Work with afghan hook. Make a ch desired length.

Row 1: Keeping all lps on hook, sk first ch from hook (lp on hook is first st), pull up a lp in each ch across: Figure 1.

To Work Lps Off: Yo hook, pull through first lp, * yo hook, pull through next 2 lps, repeat from * across until 1 lp remains: Figure 2. Lp that remains on hook always counts as first st of next row.

Row 2: Keeping all lps on hook, sk first vertical bar (lp on hook is first st), pull up a lp under next vertical bar and under each vertical bar across: Figure 3. Work lps off as before. Repeat row 2 for plain afghan stitch.

Edge Stitch:

Made at end of rows only to make a firm edge. Work as follows: Insert hook under last vertical bar and in lp at back of bar, pull up 1 lp: Figure 4.

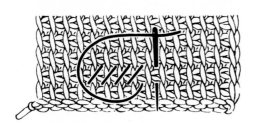

HALF CROSS-STITCH ON AFGHAN STITCH

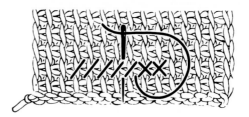

CROSS-STITCH ON AFGHAN STITCH

Twisted Cord

Method requires two people. Tie one end of yarn around pencil. Loop yarn over center of second pencil, back to and around first, and back to second, making as many strands between pencils as needed for thickness of cord; knot end to pencil. Length of yarn between pencils should be three times length of cord desired. Each person holds yarn just below pencil with one hand and twists pencil with other hand, keeping yarn taut. When yarn begins to kink, catch center over doorknob or hook. Bring pencils together for one person to hold, while other grasps center of yarn, sliding hand down at short intervals and letting yarn twist.

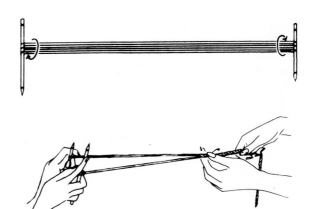

To Crochet Edge on Knitting

From right side, unless otherwise specified, work 1 sc (1 single crochet) in each stitch on bound-off or cast-on edge; work 1 sc in each knot formed on edge of each row on front or side edges; work 2 or 3 sc at corners to keep work flat. To make a single crochet, start with a loop on hook, insert hook under 2 loops of stitch on edge, draw yarn through, yarn over hook and through both loops on hook. To end off, make a sl st (slip stitch): Insert hook under both loops of stitch, catch yarn with hook and draw through stitch and loop on hook.

KNITTING NEEDLES														
U. S.	0	1	2	3	4	5	6	7	8	9	10	10½	11	13	15
English	13	12	11	10	9	8	7	6	5	4	3	2	1	00	000
Continental — mm.	2¼	2½	3	3¼	3½	4	4½	5	5½	6	6½	7	7½	8½	9

CROCHET HOOKS (ALUMINUM OR PLASTIC)										
U. S.	1/B	2/C	3/D	4/E	5/F	6/G	8/H	9/I	10/J	10½/K
English	12	11	10	9	8	7	6	5	4	2
Continental — mm.	2½	3		3½	4	4½	5	5½	6	7

How to Block

To Block Afghans: Smooth pieces out, wrong side up, on a padded surface. Using rustproof pins, place pins at top and bottom of each piece, measuring to insure correct length. Pin sides of pieces to correct width. Place pins all around outer edges, keeping patterns straight. Do not pin ribbings. **For flat pressing technique** (stockinette stitch, flat rows of crochet, other smooth surfaces): Cover with damp cloth. Lower iron gently, allowing steam to penetrate fabric. Do not press down hard or hold iron in one place long enough to dry out pressing cloth. Do not slide iron over surface. **For steam-ing technique** (mohair and other fluffy yarns, raised pattern stitches): Support weight of iron in your hand; hold as close as possible to piece without touching it and move slowly over entire piece, making sure steam penetrates fabric. If yarn is extra heavy, use a spray iron or wet pressing cloth to provide extra steam. When blocked pieces are dry, remove pins and sew pieces together. Steam-press seams from wrong side, using a steam iron or damp cloth and dry iron and same block-ing method.

How to Make a Fringe

FIG. 1   FIG. 2   FIG. 3

How to Make a Tassel

Wind yarn around cardboard cut to size of tassel desired, winding it 20 or more times around, depending on plumpness of tassel required. Tie strands tightly together around top as shown, leaving at least 3″ ends on ties; clip other end of strands. Wrap piece of yarn tightly around strands a few times, about ½″ or 1″ below tie and knot. Trim ends of tassel evenly.